ROBERT LEFFERTS

Getting a Grant in the 1980s

How to Write Successful Grant Proposals

SECOND EDITION

PRENTICE HALL PRESS • NEW YORK

Published in 1986 by Prentice Hall Press
A Division of Simon & Schuster, Inc.
Gulf + Western Building
One Gulf + Western Plaza
New York, NY 10023

Originally published by Prentice-Hall, Inc.

PRENTICE HALL PRESS is a trademark of Simon & Schuster, Inc.

Library of Congress Cataloging-in-Publication Data

Lefferts, Robert.
 Getting a grant in the 1980s.
 Rev. ed. of: Getting a grant. c1978.
 Bibliography: p.
 Includes index.
 1. Proposal writing in the social sciences.
2. Fund raising—United States. I. Title.
HV41.L413 1982   361.7′068′1   81-23360
ISBN 0-13-354522-9 (pbk.)   AACR2

Manufactured in the United States of America

10 9 8 7 6 5

Contents

Preface

I believe in the public sharing of ideas and skills. Treating ideas and skills as private property converts them into commodities for exchange rather than for social usefulness. Unfortunately, this is exactly what has happened with the skills related to proposal writing and grant seeking. These methods have often been so mystified and hidden by those who have controlled this technology that most people are intimidated by the notion of having to write a proposal. Yet, many of us do it as part of our work.

The intention of this book is to help demystify proposal writing and grant seeking by providing a set of principles, methods, and guidelines that are accessible to anyone who has basic writing skills and an understanding of the field in which they are writing. My experience in conducting seminars, institutes, and classes in proposal writing over the past fifteen years has convinced me that most people already possess the ability to write proposals of fundable quality. What they need is a set of guidelines to help them refine this ability into more effective skills. The success of the first edition of this book has confirmed my confidence in this judgment.

The material in this book is not offered as a single system or cookbook for writing effective proposals. Good proposal writers develop their own specific approaches. Proposal writing is not a linear step-by-step process of following a recipe. Rather it is the integration of ideas and of methods of presentation that require individual creativity and ingenuity, coupled with clear concise presentation. The wisest use of the principles and methods that are set forth is to pick and choose and then adapt them for one's own purposes. One should respect and have confidence in his or her own judgment and experience, as well as in the shared experience of others.

I have oriented the book to program proposals that account for the majority of grants in fields such as physical and mental health, education, welfare, employment and training, and social services. Many of the principles and methods are applicable to research proposals, and a special chapter, specifically geared to the preparation of applied research proposals, has been added to this second edition.

This edition reflects recent changes in the grants field. The increasing competition for grants in a period of limited resources increases the need for proposals to be responsive to the current interests of funders and to be directed at new funding sources. Therefore, the section of the book on locating resources has been expanded and reorganized. A section on mini-proposals has been added since it can be expected that more approaches will be made to funders, such as corporations, that may not initially require a full proposal.

I am indebted to many persons for advice, assistance, and encouragement: Rick Balkin of the Balkin Agency; John Hunger of Prentice-Hall, Inc.; Audrey Terry, who typed the original manuscript; Adrian Cabral, who encouraged me to go public with these ideas; Polly Purvis, who generously allowed me to adapt proposal materials that she prepared; Lynne Soine, who reviewed some of the early ideas; Susanne Torjussen, who did a superb secretarial job in preparing the manuscript for the second edition; Arthur Greenleigh of Greenleigh Associates; Rick Lefferts, who shared development material; and Sybil Lefferts, whose encouragement and contributions I deeply appreciate. In addition, no book in this field would be complete without acknowledging the valuable resources of the Foundation Center and the Grantsmanship Center.

Finally, I apologize for the occasional use of the term "grantsmanship" in the text, because of its sexist character. Indeed, a good deal of the language in the grants field has sex, race, and class biases indicating how this area of human endeavor simply reflects the character of many aspects of our society that must be changed. To the extent that this book will be helpful to those struggling for such change, my purpose will have been served.

ROBERT LEFFERTS
East Setauket, New York

Robert Lefferts, Ph.D., is professor at the School of Social Welfare, Health Science Center, State University of New York at Stony Brook. He has had more than twenty years of experience as an administrator and consultant for federal, state, and local health, education, and welfare agencies. His other books include *Elements of Graphics* and *Administration of Projects and Grants.*

1

Introduction

This book outlines the basic principles and skills involved in the preparation and presentation of written proposals. It is specifically directed toward proposals in the broad field of human services, including mental and physical health; education; social services; public welfare; employment and training; services for youth and the aging; cultural activities; community development; recreation; and antipoverty programs.

The book addresses the following questions:

What is a proposal?

Why are proposals increasingly important?

What are the various types of proposals?

Who prepares proposals, who receives them?

Which criteria are decisive in evaluation of proposals?

What are the essential components of a proposal?

What should be covered in each component?

What is the most effective way of presenting the material?

Which available resources are useful in preparation of the proposal?

Which available resources are useful in deciding to whom a proposal should be submitted?

What can be done to follow up after a proposal is submitted to a funding source?

The book provides guidelines for use by persons working in governmental and non-profit agencies, schools, institutions, organizations, and community groups who are seeking to acquire financial resources to support special or ongoing programs, activities, services, and studies. These financial resources are typically obtained through grants or contracts from funding sources such as federal, state, and local governmental agencies or from private foundations and corporate sources. Since most of the grants and contracts from these funding sources are provided to institutions, organizations and agencies rather than to individuals, the book emphasizes the requirements for proposals that are prepared and submitted by such organizations. It has been estimated that over one-half million agencies and organizations are receiving support from grants and contracts. Almost all of these are based on written proposals of the type described in this book.

During the 1960s and 1970s it was generally easier to obtain support from governmental and foundation sources than it is today. For one thing, the resources available to these groups have become more limited. At the same time, the number of organizations applying for grants has increased. In addition, allocating agencies have become more critical in their assessment of proposed programs. In part, this is due to the more limited resources, but it is also the result of some bad experiences in funding proposed activities that never produced the results that were promised. Furthermore, allocating organizations have become more sophisticated and have developed criteria and review methods that enable them to examine proposed programs more carefully.

All of these factors have resulted in an increasing emphasis on the written proposal as an important basis for making judgments regarding the allocation of funds. This neither means that a good proposal automatically results in obtaining a grant nor that the quality of the proposal is the only factor taken into consideration in deciding on a grant award. Political, personal, ideological, and other factors always influence decision making in government and foundations, just as they influence decision making in all other aspects of American life. Grantsmanship, proposal writing, and presentation are not activities that can rely on the operation of some meritocracy, in which rewards are objectively distributed on the basis of merit alone. For this reason, one can receive endless and often contradictory advice from "experts" on how best to obtain a grant. Nevertheless, practically every effort to obtain a grant will require the preparation and presentation of a written proposal. The quality of that proposal is almost always a critical factor, if not *the* critical factor, which contributes to success or failure in obtaining a grant.

Proposal writing is both an art and a technical craft. There are, of course, many ways to organize and prepare a proposal. Every proposal writer has his or her own style and method of presentation. It is not the purpose of this book to make all proposals look alike, or to reduce the creativity involved in writing a proposal to a technical exercise, devoid of personal involvement. There is no sure-fire set of instructions to guarantee a good proposal. Nevertheless, there are certain principles and methods that can serve to refine and improve the ability to prepare more convincing proposals. It is toward the refinement and enhancement of these skills, both of new and of experienced proposal writers, that this book is addressed.

In addition to the necessity for a high-quality effective proposal, another problem is faced by organizations seeking grants. This is the question of sending the application for funds to the appropriate source. Perhaps no division of the human services field is characterized by a greater proliferation of potential resources than the grant-making sector. There are more than 25,000 foundations and thousands of federal, state, and local governmental programs that provide grants in this field. Moreover, a large number of corporations provide grants for research, training, and public service programs through corporate gifts and corporate foundations. Proposal writers must develop guidelines for making decisions as to where to seek funds. Fortunately, there are a number of resources available for identification of potential funders. These resources, and suggestions for their use, are also included in this book. Given the necessary resources, most grant seekers will be able to figure out the best places to obtain funds. We therefore stress resources, principles, and skills instead of giving any magic system or formula to assist persons and organizations in dealing with the confusing and often frustrating problem of identifying potential funders.

2

What Is a Proposal?

A proposal is a plan presented for acceptance, according to Webster. The word is composed of the Latin word *pro*, which means for, or in favor of, and the French word *poser*, meaning to set forth. A proposal is thus a positive statement, never a negative one. It sets forth a program or set of activities.

One cannot properly make a proposal *against* something. A counterproposal may be directed against some idea, but it is a positive assertion of an alternative.

A proposal always requires two parties, since it must be made to someone else who either accepts, rejects, or modifies it. Thus, when writing a proposal, one must keep in mind that it is being written for presentation to another party in order to gain its acceptance. Does a proposal therefore require the compromise of one's principles or values in order to please the funder? It certainly does not. However, it does require presentation with a sufficient degree of clarity and persuasiveness to be convincing. Also, the proposal must be in tune with the needs and interests of the other party, that is, of the funder. In order to communicate effectively with a funder, the proposal must be consistent with the funder's interests.

A proposal serves five functions. It is a written representation of a program, it is a request, it is an instrument of persuasion, it is a promise and a commitment, and it is a plan. It is useful for proposal writers to be aware of these functions, since each function has certain implications for the preparation and presentation of the proposal. An outline of the functions follows.

PROGRAM REPRESENTATION

As we said, the first function of a proposal is that it is a written statement that represents a particular program, activity or project that an organization, group, or individual seeks to undertake. It is part of the process of program planning, program development, and resource acquisition that takes place in all human service organizations. The proposal is a reflection of the organization's total program-development process. It represents, in writing, to the requesting agency and to the funder alike a specific set of activities that are part of the organization's total development.

REQUEST

The second function of a proposal is that it is a request for the allocation of resources from a funding source. This means that the proposal should very clearly convey the exact extent of and the reason for the request.

The tone of the proposal is important if it is to command the respect and attention of the funder. Proposals that appear to be begging for funds are not respected by funders, since they give the impression that the applicant is not sure of the value of the proposed work. On the other hand, proposals that reflect a tone of arrogance are also to be avoided, since they may negate the possibility for the kind of mutuality of interest and working relationship that most funders seek.

PERSUASION

The third function of a proposal is that it is an instrument of persuasion; it seeks to persuade some person or organization to support and legitimate the proposed program by allocating resources to that program. In this sense the proposal is also a political document, because particular strategies are used in the process of persuasion to convince a real or potential adversary to become an ally. To some extent, proposal writers view funders as adversaries until they come through with the sought-after grant. Furthermore, the proposal, once it is funded, implies the approval of the funding source for the idea and activities that the proposal represents. This necessitates a degree of ethical as well as fiscal accountability on the part of the applicant with regard to the funding agency, organization, or foundation.

PROMISE

The fourth function of a proposal is that it is a promise. It is the applicant's promise to the funding source to do certain things, in a certain way, during a specified period of time, and at a given cost. Frequently, especially when federal, state, and local governmental agencies are involved, the proposal is made part of a legal contract. Thus, it becomes a formal commitment that legally binds the proponent in exchange for the funds received. In view of this, it is not unusual for funding sources to impose various conditions and responsibilities on the grant recipient. Usually these requirements call at least for periodic progress reports. Sometimes, however, they may also call for certain changes or modifications in the proposed program.

In general, chances of being funded are improved by straightforwardness in describing the nature of the proposed program. It is not advisable to "psyche out" funders in terms of their politics. Conservative funders have supported radical programs. Liberal funders support conservative proposals. Whatever the politics of a proposal, one should stay away from rhetoric and inflammatory language. Facts and documentation must be stressed. Those aspects of the proposed program that challenge accepted ideas and practices must be low-keyed and described precisely. However, one should not hesitate to challenge ideas, since this is the essence of innovation—which is an important consideration to many funders.

PLAN

The final function of a proposal is that it is a plan that serves as a set of guidelines for the organization and implementation of the program. As such, the proposal specifies the activities to be carried out, the way in which they will be accomplished, the number and type of staff needed, the organization of the staff, the management of the program, the required equipment and facilities, the cost of each item in the budget, and the starting and completion dates of each activity. Proposal writing, therefore, is really a major aspect of program planning and development. A good proposal reflects good program planning and is a useful tool for program management.

In light of the foregoing, the importance of good proposals cannot be stressed too strongly. One additional factor should also be remembered. One is almost always competing with others to obtain the funds sought for the program. While exact figures are not available, at least a million proposals are written and submitted each year for funding in the broad human services field. These proposals are mostly submitted to federal, state, and local governmental agencies and to foundations. About $30 billion is allocated each year in response to proposals.[1] At best, however, only one out of ten proposals that are submitted eventually gets funded. The quality of the proposal is not the only factor that affects a funding decision, but it is one of the most critical aspects of gaining support.

Different people begin the proposal-writing process in different ways, depending on their general approach to problem solving, decision making, and planning. Some people start with a general idea, concept, or purpose and then proceed to make it more specific. This is called *deductive* thinking. Others start with very specific program ideas and then expand these into an overall plan and set of objectives. This is called *inductive* thinking. Most people tend to go back and forth from general to specific, from specific to general. This means that one should expect to make a number of revisions in the proposal during the process of preparation. We shall provide guidelines to proposal writing that can be utilized in both deductive and inductive approaches. When the proposal is finally completed, it should be carefully edited and gone over to make sure that it meets the criteria outlined later.

Before describing the guidelines for the contents of a proposal and the way of presentation, it is important to review the different types of proposals and the criteria to be used in assessing the effectiveness of a proposal.

[1]Most of this is in governmental grants and contracts. The total amount granted from the approximately 25,000 foundations in the United States is around $2 billion; and another $2 billion comes from corporate sources.

3

Types of Proposals

There are five principal types of proposals in the human services field:

Program proposals—to offer a particular set of services to individuals, families, groups, or communities.

Research proposals—to study a problem, group, or organization or to evaluate a service.

Planning proposals—to provide planning and coordination with respect to a problem, group of agencies or organizations, or set of services.

Training proposals—to provide training and education to individuals, groups, and organizations.

Technical-assistance proposals—to offer assistance to groups, agencies, organizations, and communities in establishing and implementing programs, research, planning, training, or administration.

Most proposals submitted by human service organizations are program proposals; therefore, that type of proposal is emphasized in this book. In addition, because research proposals have specialized characteristics, a separate chapter is devoted to research proposals. Any particular proposal may, of course, contain a combination of two or more of these types. For example, a proposal may include a set of program activities and a training program. A proposal may include a certain amount of planning, to be followed by the implementation of a service program. A program proposal often includes an evaluation component, which is a form of research.

Regardless of the type of proposal being prepared, the same general guidelines apply, although there will naturally be differences in the specifics and context. For example, a research proposal should include a research design that describes the data to be collected, the methods to be used in collecting and analyzing the data, and the hypotheses to be tested, whereas a program proposal includes a program design that specifies each program activity, the number and characteristics of the persons to be served, and the service delivery method.

Another distinction is whether the proposal is made for a "demonstration" or for an ongoing program project. A proposal should be presented as a demonstration if one or more of the following facts apply:

a. The funding source, such as a government program, is required by its regulations to fund only demonstrations or special projects or the foundation has restrictions on making funds available for ongoing or regular programs. In such a case the proposal should be set up as a special project or as a demonstration.

b. The proposed activities include a clear set of methods, approaches, or strategies that are being piloted in order to test or demonstrate their strengths and weaknesses.

c. It is evident that the proposal is a major departure from what is considered to be the routine ongoing operation of the agency.

Proposals may be either solicited or unsolicited. A solicited proposal is prepared in response to a formal, written "request for proposals" known as an RFP. These requests are prepared and sent to prospective agencies and organizations (both profit and nonprofit) by the particular federal, state, or local agency that is to provide the funds and contract for the service. In addition to RFPs, funding sources often send out "program announcements" and "program guidelines" that describe the availability of funds for various purposes. Often an opportunity for funding is located in the Commerce Business Daily, a government publication listing the availability of RFPs and program announcements from federal governmental programs.

Unsolicited proposals are not prepared in response to a formal RFP.

They are sent to funding agencies and foundations known to support the kind of program that is proposed.

Some governmental funders also distinguish between technical proposals, which include all programmatic and organizational aspects of the proposal, and business proposals, which include all budgetary and pricing information.

Occasionally an organization may have a unique capability to carry out a project and will therefore be selected by a funder as the so-called sole source to receive a contract. In such a case, there is no competition with other organizations, but a proposal acceptable to the funder must still be prepared.

Proposals may seek to cover either operating costs or construction costs of a program or project. Many funders do not support capital costs, such as construction of facilities or renovation of offices. Proposals of this kind should be very selectively submitted.

GRANTS AND CONTRACTS

The two main ways in which foundations, government agencies, and other funding sources support outside organizations are through grants and contracts. Both these support mechanisms are utilized to define the conditions, requirements, and expectations of the funder and recipient. Thus, they both guide the nature of the relationship between funders and recipients. There are some significant differences between these two mechanisms that are important to understand, since they can not only influence certain aspects of the proposal itself but may also affect the manner in which funds are managed by recipients after they are awarded.

The major difference is that contracts are generally much more specific about the particular services to be provided by the grantee and that they specify the final results or products that are expected. If a proposal is in response to an RFP, one can usually expect the award to be in the form of a contract. If, on the other hand, a proposal is in response to a program announcement or submitted without having been solicited, the funds will be awarded as a grant. Grant awards may specify the general services to be provided but often may not require a specific product. Applications for grants from government funders usually require completion of application forms that cover both program and budget information. This is usually not the case with foundation grant awards for which a narrative proposal and budget are sufficient. Foundations seldom use formal contracts as the vehicle for supporting programs; instead, they use award letters and letters of agreement.

For contracts from federal and other government agencies the main forms utilized are related to financial information and certification of business, administrative, and employment practices. For awards from the government to a profit-making organization or agency a formal contract is normally negotiated.

Many proposal writers and administrators believe that, from the standpoint of the grantee, a grant is preferable to a contract. Supposedly a grant results in more flexibility for the grantee. In addition, grants are not monitored by funding agencies as closely as contracts.

There are a variety of different types of grants and contracts that are used by funders to convey funds to grantees. These mechanisms provide for different arrangements with respect to the conditions under which funds are conveyed and expended by the recipient. Contracts include cost-plus, cost-reimbursable, and cost-sharing contracts. Grants are classified according to purpose. They include program grants, research grants, training grants, planning grants, construction grants, and grants-in-aid. The differences among these contract and grant mechanisms are defined in the Glossary.

4

Criteria for Evaluating Proposals

Most funding sources, including almost all federal agencies, apply formal criteria in evaluating proposals. One can use these same criteria for self-evaluation of the proposal prior to its submission to a funder. A funder may be requested to provide the criteria and priority statements used, since these are usually public information.

The criteria used by funders vary, of course; however, the following list represents those that are most frequently used. Sometimes they are applied very formally and points are awarded for each criterion when the proposal is evaluated. For example, the criterion of clarity may be worth 25 points and each proposal received is given up to 25 points, depending on the judgment of the individual or panel that reviews it. In other cases the criteria are not made explicit and are not applied formally but are simply guidelines in the mind of the reviewers.

One can evaluate his or her own proposal against the following nine criteria:

a. Clarity

b. Completeness

c. Responsiveness
d. Internal consistency
e. External consistency
f. Understanding of the problem and service methods
g. Capability
h. Efficiency and accountability
i. Realism

These criteria are explained in a general way below. It should be remembered that, when applied by a specific funder to a specific proposal, they are used in a more specific sense. For example, if the proposal is for a program in the area of juvenile delinquency, the funder wants the applicant to demonstrate an understanding of the specifics of the juvenile-delinquency problem and of the delivery of services or conduct of research in this field.

CLARITY

The proposal must be clearly written and organized so that it can be readily followed and easily understood. The style of writing and organization of material should be as simple as possible. Complicated sentence structure, verbiage, abstractions that are not clarified with examples, long sentences, and a great deal of cross-referencing should be avoided.

It is important to avoid jargon whose meaning is ambiguous, but one should use a certain amount of the generally understood technical or professional language relevant to the area covered by the proposal. One should be convinced, however, that the funding reviewers also are familiar with this language and use it.

Clarity is enhanced by a logical flow of ideas and by the use of headings and subheadings that serve to break up the text and also describe what is to follow.

It cannot be assumed that the funder will understand what is intended unless the proposal includes a full explanation. The writer has to ask "Will someone unfamiliar with my organization have a *clear picture* of what is being proposed from reading the proposal?" After the proposal is complete, one must identify what kinds of questions a funder may ask about the proposal and have two or three other people review it critically. Thereupon the proposal has to undergo revision to cover the answers to the anticipated questions.

COMPLETENESS

The proposal must include all the components and elements that will be outlined in Chapters 5 and 6. If the proposal is being written in response to an RFP, program announcement, regulations, or guidelines one should be sure that it covers every item that is specified. It should cover all relevant points, so that the funding agency does not have any major unanswered questions about purpose, objectives, need, activities, staffing, organization, timing, or budget request. Use of the words "etc." or "and so forth" must be avoided, since this may be construed to indicate that the writer really does not know the complete range of material to be presented.

RESPONSIVENESS

Proposals must be responsive to the requirements of the funding agency and must also be responsive to a documented problem and need.

Responsiveness to Funding Agency Requirements and Purposes

Proposals to government funding agencies must be responsive to all the substantive specifications regarding both format and content set forth in the RFP, program-announcement, guidelines, regulations, and legislation relevant to the program under which funding is sought. They must also be responsive to the general interests and purposes of the funder to whom they are submitted. The information needed to assure that a proposal is responsive to these requirements is provided by examination of the legislative authority, rules, regulations, program guidelines, goals, and objectives of the governmental funding programs concerned.

Some foundations also have written guidelines that proposals must meet. In addition, information to enhance responsiveness to the interests of a particular foundation can be provided by examination of foundation reports and other materials. These reports are available in the Foundation Center Library, which has offices in New York City and other cities throughout the country. These are listed in the appendix. Corporate funders also have special interests, and corporate grants are made to reflect favorably on the corporation. Proposals to corporations should, therefore, show a connection between the proposed project and the interests of the corporation.

Responsiveness to Need

The proposal should also demonstrate that it is responding to a real and documented need in the community, among the group to be served, and/or in the general field. This need should be comprehensively documented, following the guidelines in Chapter 5. The proposal will be strengthened by showing that the proposed program is responsive to the interests of those who will be involved. Letters of endorsement and results of surveys and community meetings can serve to document responsiveness to need.

INTERNAL CONSISTENCY

All parts of the proposal should be related to and consistent with each other. For example, the kinds of activities proposed should be logically consistent with the objectives that are set forth. Similarly, the proposed staff should be of sufficient size and quality to deliver the proposed services. Statements about need should be directly relevant to the specific program activities that are being proposed.

EXTERNAL CONSISTENCY

The proposal should recognize both the generally known and accepted ideas in the particular field and the program approaches, activities, and methods that are believed to be effective. If alternative definitions of the problem and alternative service strategies and methods are proposed, they should be justified in terms of a systematic critique of the dominant ideas and methods. This, in effect, is a way to enhance the innovative aspects of the proposal and to demonstrate at the same time familiarity with the field.

UNDERSTANDING
OF THE PROBLEM
AND SERVICE METHODS

It is important to indicate a thorough understanding of the nature of the problem that the program addresses. In addition, the proposal should show one's understanding of the way in which the proposed services must be delivered. Most importantly, it must have an effective plan to carry out the proposed activities. A proposal is also strengthened by indicating that one understands the barriers, problems, and difficulties that must be overcome in order to effectively provide the proposed services and achieve the objectives.

CAPABILITY

A major criterion to funders is evidence of the capability of the organization to successfully carry out the activities it promises to implement in its written proposal. This can be conveyed in a number of ways, particularly by the quality of the proposal itself and by demonstrating familiarity with the problem, the relevant literature, the service-delivery methods, and other similar programs. Setting forth the qualifications of the proposed staff, or the experience and resources of the agency involved, is likewise important in emphasizing capability. Funders are usually concerned with the applicant's prior work or "track record" of successful operation.

It is often advisable to include a separate "capability statement" with the proposal. This should take the form of an attachment or appendix. Letters of endorsement from key organizations and authorities may also be attached and referred to in the proposal. Finally, evidence of the applicant's plans and ability to assure continuance of the project in the future serves to convey capability to a funder.

EFFICIENCY AND ACCOUNTABILITY

Funders want to be assured that programs will be efficiently managed and effectively executed. Plans for the administration and organization of the program activities, staff, and committees are ways to indicate ability to efficiently implement the program. Assurance of accountability to the community, a larger institution, and the funder are other factors that enhance efficiency. A detailed timetable is important as well. Other ways to stress efficiency are to compare the cost of the program with the cost of alternative programs; indicate the cost of the problem to the community; and show a favorable relationship between the budgeted expenses and the activities for the number of people to be served (the so-called unit costs).

The accountability factor of the proposal can be strengthened by indicating the kinds of managerial and financial systems and controls that will be employed; by showing how advisory boards and committees will be utilized; and by providing a description of regular reports to the membership, other institutions, and the funder.

REALISM

A proposal should be realistic. No more than can really be achieved and delivered in the way of objectives and program activities should be promised. The proposal should be geared to the realities of the number of people that can actually be served.

The dollar request has to be consistent with the amount of money that may be available from the funder. Chapters 7 and 8 will suggest certain specific resources and techniques for making a realistic assessment of potential resources.

For additional reading about the above criteria we suggest the following articles of the *Grantsmanship Center News* (1015 West Olympic Boulevard, Los Angeles, California 90015): "How Foundations Review Proposals and Make Grants," "Researching Foundations," and "An Inside Look at How the Government Evaluates Proposals."

A number of ideas relevant to foundation proposals have been set forth by F. Lee Jacquette and Barbara I. Jacquette, in "What Makes a Good Proposal," *The Foundation News*, January 1973. Reprints are available from the Foundation Center, 888 Seventh Avenue, New York 10019. This article is specifically geared to proposals submitted to foundations. It stresses the need for a clear summary of the proposed accomplishment, an explanation of the need for the proposed program and of its difference from programs worked out by others, a description of the people to be involved including their biographies and qualifications, presentation of a realistic financing scheme and of an appropriate set of organizational arrangements. According to this article, most foundations assess proposals using the following criteria:

Competence of persons involved

Feasibility and realism of the proposal

Importance and utility of the venture to the community or to society

Originality and creativity of the proposed venture

Appropriateness of the project to the foundation's policy and program focus

Prospects for leverage and pattern-making effects

Need for foundation support

Soundness of the budget

Persistence, dedication, and commitment of the proposers

Provision of objective evaluation of results, where feasible

Another helpful article is "What Will a Foundation Look for When You

Submit a Grant Proposal" by Robert A. Mayer. It is available from the Foundation Center. Mayer says that foundation staff members look for the following in a proposal:

> Does the proposal fit within the foundation's program interests?
>
> Is the type of support requested of the kind the foundation gives (for example, the covering of operating deficits, construction, or special projects)?
>
> Does the project have value, a transferral potential, an impact on need, or an intrinsic value of its own from which others might benefit?
>
> Is it aimed at building organizations in areas in which the foundation has institution-building purposes?
>
> Is the cost, timetable, and future financing plan realistic?
>
> Does the organization have the leadership, experience, and re-sources to accomplish the objectives?

In 1974, the results of a study of criteria used by 100 government and foundation grantors were published. Among twenty different criteria, five were rated as highest in importance in making decisions about grants for community projects. These five factors were:[2]

> Consistency of the purpose of the project with the funders' purposes
>
> Full, concise, convincing documentation of need
>
> Assurance of the financial and legal accountability of the recipient
>
> Evidence of the competence of the recipient to carry out the project
>
> Assurance of feasibility in terms of adequate resources to accom-plish the objectives of the project

Some funders use a very brief and rather specific set of criteria upon which they base their assessment of a proposal. For example, a government anti-crime grant program listed the following criteria:

1. Clear definition of objectives
2. Crime-analysis data on the community that demonstrate a need for the program
3. Endorsement of the proposal by the local police department
4. Demonstrate coordination and involvement of the police in the program

[2]Ted H. Townsend, "Criteria Grantors Use in Assessing Proposals," *Foundation News,* March, 1974, pp. 33–38.

5.   Specific qualifications of the applicant to perform the projects

Another federal program indicates it rates proposals according to the following criteria:

1.   Needs and objectives—10 points
2.   Evidence of private sector involvement—0 to 30 points
3.   Cost effectiveness and reasonableness—0 to 10 points
4.   Demand for occupational choices identified for training—0 to 20 points
5.   Ability of applicant to provide effective programming—0 to 30 points

From experience with government and foundation reviewers it is evident that, in addition to the general criteria outlined earlier, there are also a number of more specific items that reviewers tend to look for in a proposal. These include:

1.   The importance or significance of the project in terms of documented need, the extent to which the project will meet this need, and the number and characteristics of the people to be served.
2.   The extent to which the project involves the cooperation of other community resources, both public and private, and evidence that duplication and overlapping of services is avoided.
3.   The specificity with which objectives are set forth and the suitability of the proposed methods or activities as means to accomplish the objectives.
4.   The clear description of the proposed tasks and the competence of the proposers to make good on their promises.
5.   The suitability and soundness of proposed evaluation techniques, particularly in terms of the kinds of measurements that will be made, the feasibility of obtaining data adequate for making such measurements, and clarity with respect to the question which specific evaluation issues will, and which will not be answered as a result of the evaluation. There is a tendency for program-proposal writers to hedge more in relationship to evaluation than to any other section of the proposal, and reviewers recognize this.
6.   The evidence that the proposed project has a relationship to other local, state, or national programs with which the government funding agency also has a relationship or interest.
7.   The possibility that the proposed program can be sold by reviewers to other officials in the funding agency who also need to approve it.

8. The reasonableness of the budget, its technical presentation and accuracy, and the probability of continuing support. An increasing amount of attention is given to judgments about the relationship of costs to benefits and effectiveness. These judgments are made in terms of whether unit costs are reasonable and in line with similar programs, and whether the proposed program is worth its costs in relation to the probability of achieving its program objectives and its impact on the problem.

A variety of forms and instructions are used among governmental proposal reviewers. Often reviewers are asked to make a general rating or recommendation regarding each proposal such as approve, approve with provisions or qualifications, disapprove, or defer action. Reviewers also rate various aspects of the proposal awarding points or using scales. For example, reviewers may be asked to rate "the significance of the problem addressed" on a five-point scale of 1–5; similarly, other aspects, such as the adequacy of procedures and methods, the qualifications of staff, and the extent to which budget costs are proportionate to expected results may be rated on point scales.

In preparing a proposal, the writer should have all the foregoing criteria and questions in mind and should reexamine each component of the proposal to see if it can be strengthened to more nearly conform to these criteria.

Proposal writers should not be overly mystified or overwhelmed by these criteria. For one thing, they are really not that complicated, since they all reflect common-sense questions, which anyone would ask when faced with making a decision about providing resources to another party. In addition, it should be recognized that the decision-making process among funding agencies is not always as orderly, technical, and rational as the discussion of criteria might imply or as funders' formal descriptions of their decision-making process may sound. A good deal of personal judgment, not reflected in formal criteria but rather based on values and politics affecting the funder, can come into play.[3]

---

[3]In the case of foundations, for example, a study has shown a great deal of variability in the way decisions are made and approved. See Peter G. Peterson, *Foundations, Private Giving, and Public Policy: Report and Recommendations of the Commission on Foundations and Private Philanthropy* (Chicago: University of Chicago Press, 1970).

5

Components
of a Proposal

A proposal should include the following seventeen components:

Letter of Transmittal
Title Page
Table of Contents
Summary
Introductory Statements
Statement of the Problem and Need
Purpose
Objectives, Goals, or Strategy
Conceptual Framework or Rationale
Program Design and Activities
Organizational and Administrative Structure and Plan
Staffing Plan
Timetable
Evaluation

Budget

Capability Statement

Supporting Documents

Principles and methods for preparing and presenting the material for each of these components will be taken up separately in the following sections. In many cases, governmental funding agencies require submission of a proposal using their forms. Samples of some of these forms are included later in this chapter. Most forms call for information similar to the above-mentioned components, but not necessarily in the same sequence.

The question is often raised, "What is the most important part of the proposal?" Naturally, all parts of the proposal are important, because it can be rejected by a funder for a weakness in any section. Thus, the question should really be, "Which section of the proposal most often contributes to rejection?" In a study by the National Institute of Health in 1969 the main two reasons for rejection were either weakness in the approach to the problem or lack of sufficient confidence in the competence of the proposers. Although this was a study primarily of research proposals, it can be safely assumed that similar reasons would prevail for the rejection of human service program proposals. This suggests that the major weakness of many program proposals lies in the manner in which the program plan and activities and the proposers' capability and staffing plans are presented. We shall therefore not only present sound principles and methods of proposal preparation but we shall also call attention to some of the more frequent errors of proposal writers that provide a basis for rejection.

Letter of Transmittal and Title Page

LETTER OF TRANSMITTAL

The letter of transmittal or covering letter formally submits the proposal of the organization to the funder. It should include the following:

Name of the organization submitting the proposal

Concise summary of the problem involved, need, objectives, and proposed program approach

Brief statement of the organization's interest in the project and its capability and experience

Address and name of whom to contact for further information and indication of willingness to provide it

Figure 1.   Letter of Transmittal.

March 31, 19___

Ms. Mary Smith
Famous Foundation
One Washington Street
Grantsville, U.S.A.

Dear Ms. Smith:

The ABC Organization is pleased to submit the enclosed proposal to provide a juvenile-delinquency prevention program for teen-age youths in Sea County. This program is in keeping with the expressed goal of your foundation to support alternative programs for youths. The purpose of the program is to demonstrate the effectiveness of providing a range of social, health, educational, and employment services for teen-agers who come to the attention of the police. This program, endorsed by the police department, would be an alternative to these youths entering the criminal-justice system. We believe that to divert youths from the generally unsatisfactory effects of detention, probation, and institutionalization will serve to prevent a continuation of antisocial behavior for many youths.

The ABC Organization has provided a wide variety of services to individuals and families in Sea City since 1947. As an incorporated nonprofit agency we have demonstrated in the past our capability to successfully carry out similar demonstrations of alternative services for the aged, unwed mothers, released prisoners, and discharged mental patients. We have a highly qualified and capable staff, which has considerable experience in operating community-based alternative services. Our Board of Directors is a highly committed group of men and women. They represent the major interests in our community and have many years' experience in establishing policies to assure efficient and effective operations

The enclosed proposal outlines, in detail, the objectives, services, staffing, management plan, and budget for this proposed program. We would be glad to discuss this proposal with you and are willing to provide any additional information that you might want. We shall look forward to hearing from you.

Sincerely yours,

Virginia Jones, President
Enc.

In some instances, federal RFPs require information as to the writer of the proposal and to the length of time for which the proposal and the budget can be considered firm commitments. The reason is that it can take several months before a proposal is approved. Some government forms do not call for a letter of transmittal, but it is usually a good idea to include one anyway.

The letter of transmittal should be on the letterhead stationery of the organization. The letterhead should not be elaborate; however, it should convey confidence by indicating that the organization is incorporated, by listing the board of directors (if any), by showing affiliation with a larger or national institution, and by showing the organization's address and telephone number. The letter should be signed by an appropriate organizational official, whose title conveys his or her authority.

The letter of transmittal is the first part of the proposal to which a funder is exposed. It can set the tone for the review of the remainder of the proposal. It should be brief, clear, neat, and properly addressed, covering one, two, or three pages at the most. If the proposal is rather short, the letter of transmittal may also include a brief (two-to-four paragraph) summary of the proposal. If the proposal is longer, a summary should be part of it. Figure 1 is a sample of a typical letter of transmittal.

TITLE PAGE

A separate title page or cover enhances the appearance of the proposal, adds to its clarity, and makes the proposal more credible. The title may be repeated at the top of the first page of the narrative text, but it is preferable to also have a single title page showing minimally:

> Title of the proposal
> Descriptive subtitle if necessary
> Name and address of the organization submitting the proposal
> Date prepared or submitted
> Name of the funding organization to whom the proposal is being
>   submitted (optional)

If a title is used that is an acronym, that is, a combination of first letters of component words, a descriptive subtitle must definitely be given. In addition, a title like "Operation Help" does not provide, by itself, any understanding of what the proposal is about. A subtitle, such as "A

Program to Develop Peer Counseling among Handicapped Youths," clarifies the project. The more direct, clear, and descriptive the title is, the better.

Some proposal writers suggest to include on the title page the scheduled dates of operation of the proposed project, and to show the total amount of funds being requested.

For proposals to government programs that provide forms as part of their application material, a title page is usually not necessary. Figure 2 is a sample title page.

Proposal to Establish
A Youth-Delinquency Prevention Program

Submitted to
The Famous Foundation
by the
ABC Organization
1 Washington Street
Grantsville, U.S.A.

Total Request $100,000

Figure 2.   Sample Title Page.

Figure 3 shows an example of the kind of information often required by federal funding agencies as the first page of an application kit. This example is the "Standard Form 424" required of all intergovernmental programs. In effect, it represents a title page or summary page of the proposal. Detailed programmatic and financial information elaborating on each item is usually required on additional forms.

FEDERAL ASSISTANCE	2. APPLI-CANT'S APPLI-CATION	a. NUMBER	3. STATE APPLICA-TION IDENTI-FIER	a. NUMBER

1. TYPE OF ACTION (Mark appropriate box)
- ☐ PREAPPLICATION
- ☐ APPLICATION
- ☐ NOTIFICATION OF INTENT (Opt.)
- ☐ REPORT OF FEDERAL ACTION

2. APPLICANT'S APPLICATION
b. DATE   Year month day   19
Leave Blank

3. STATE APPLICATION IDENTIFIER
b. DATE ASSIGNED   Year month day   19

4. LEGAL APPLICANT/RECIPIENT
- a. Applicant Name :
- b. Organization Unit :
- c. Street/P.O. Box :
- d. City :
- e. County :
- f. State :
- g. ZIP Code:
- h. Contact Person (Name & telephone No.) :

5. FEDERAL EMPLOYER IDENTIFICATION NO.

6. PRO-GRAM (From Federal Catalog)
- a. NUMBER | | | ● | | |
- b. TITLE

7. TITLE AND DESCRIPTION OF APPLICANT'S PROJECT

8. TYPE OF APPLICANT/RECIPIENT
A—State
B—Interstate
C—Substate District
D—County
E—City
F—School District
G—Special Purpose District
H—Community Action Agency
I—Higher Educational Institution
J—Indian Tribe
K—Other (Specify):
Enter appropriate letter ☐

9. TYPE OF ASSISTANCE
A—Basic Grant
B—Supplemental Grant
C—Loan
D—Insurance
E—Other
Enter appropriate letter(s) ☐☐

10. AREA OF PROJECT IMPACT (Names of cities, counties, States, etc.)

11. ESTIMATED NUMBER OF PERSONS BENEFITING

12. TYPE OF APPLICATION
A—New   C—Revision   E—Augmentation
B—Renewal   D—Continuation
Enter appropriate letter ☐

13. PROPOSED FUNDING
	$	.00
a. FEDERAL	$	.00
b. APPLICANT		.00
c. STATE		.00
d. LOCAL		.00
e. OTHER		.00
f. TOTAL	$	.00

14. CONGRESSIONAL DISTRICTS OF:
a. APPLICANT   b. PROJECT

16. PROJECT START DATE Year month day   19

17. PROJECT DURATION Months

18. ESTIMATED DATE TO BE SUBMITTED TO FEDERAL AGENCY ► Year month day   19

15. TYPE OF CHANGE (For 12c or 12e)
A—Increase Dollars
B—Decrease Dollars
C—Increase Duration
D—Decrease Duration
E—Cancellation
F—Other (Specify):
Enter appropriate letter(s) ☐☐

19. EXISTING FEDERAL IDENTIFICATION NUMBER

20. FEDERAL AGENCY TO RECEIVE REQUEST (Name, City, State, ZIP code)

21. REMARKS ADDED
☐ Yes ☐ No

22. THE APPLICANT CERTIFIES THAT ►
a. To the best of my knowledge and belief, data in this preapplication/application are true and correct, the document has been duly authorized by the governing body of the applicant and the applicant will comply with the attached assurances if the assistance is approved.

b. If required by OMB Circular A-95 this application was submitted, pursuant to instructions therein, to appropriate clearinghouses and all responses are attached.
(1)
(2)
(3)

	No response	Response attached
	☐	☐
	☐	☐
	☐	☐

23. CERTIFYING REPRESENTATIVE
a. TYPED NAME AND TITLE   b. SIGNATURE   c. DATE SIGNED   Year month day   19

24. AGENCY NAME

25. APPLICATION RECEIVED Year month day   19

26. ORGANIZATIONAL UNIT

27. ADMINISTRATIVE OFFICE

28. FEDERAL APPLICATION IDENTIFICATION

29. ADDRESS

30. FEDERAL GRANT IDENTIFICATION

31. ACTION TAKEN
- ☐ a. AWARDED
- ☐ b. REJECTED
- ☐ c. RETURNED FOR AMENDMENT
- ☐ d. DEFERRED
- ☐ e. WITHDRAWN

32. FUNDING
a. FEDERAL	$	.00
b. APPLICANT		.00
c. STATE		.00
d. LOCAL		.00
e. OTHER		.00
f. TOTAL	$	.00

33. ACTION DATE ► Year month day   19

34. STARTING DATE Year month day   19

35. CONTACT FOR ADDITIONAL INFORMATION (Name and telephone number)

35. ENDING DATE Year month day   19

37. REMARKS ADDED
☐ Yes ☐ No

38. FEDERAL AGENCY A-95 ACTION
a. In taking above action, any comments received from clearinghouses were considered. If agency response is due under provisions of Part 1, OMB Circular A-95, it has been or is being made.

b. FEDERAL AGENCY A-95 OFFICIAL (Name and telephone no.)

Figure 3. Information often requested by federal funding agencies.

Table of Contents
and the Use of Headings

A separate page must be used to list a table of contents that shows the title of each major section and subsection of the proposal and the number of the page where the section begins. The table of contents should follow the title page.

It helps to use an outline format in presenting the proposal by giving each major section a roman numeral, each subsection a capital letter, each heading under a subsection an arabic number, and each heading under this a lower-case letter. An example of the use of headings and subheadings for a section of the proposal organized in this manner follows:

IV. Program Activities
    A. General Approach
    B. Counseling Programs
        1. Individual Counseling
            a. Youths
            b. Adults
        2. Group Counseling
            a. Youth Groups
            b. Family Groups
    C. Day-Care Program
        1. Daily Schedule of Activities
        2. Eligibility for Service
            a. Financial Eligibility
            b. Age Eligibility
        3. Parent Involvement

Each heading should be descriptive of the narrative material that follows and not only convey the essence of that material but also represent the central concept or theme presented in that particular section. The format of headings used throughout the narrative proposal is repeated in the table of contents; page numbers are added. Thus, the table of contents for the example shown above would appear as follows:

The table of contents is a way of presenting to the reader an overall picture of the topics covered in the proposal. When carefully selected headings are used, it can make a major contribution to conveying a sense of the coherence, unity, and clarity of the proposal. A frequent mistake is that too little attention is paid to the choice of headings and subheadings. The tendency is to see this as a relatively unimportant aspect of the proposal. Nothing could be further from the truth. This part of the proposal represents an important consideration taken into account by funders, that is, the extent to which the applicant can present material in an orderly fashion.

Summaries

When the narrative proposal exceeds seven or eight pages (and most proposals do), a summary or abstract of one or two pages should be included. The summary should cover, in brief form, the highlights of the material in each section of the proposal. If the letter of transmittal has an adequate summary, a formal separate summary section may be omitted. However, for proposals of ten to fifteen pages or more, it may be impossible to include an adequate summary in the letter of transmittal.

Sometimes, when organizations are exploring funding possibilities, a summary of three to six pages is prepared as a prospectus. This may be sent to funders, usually foundations, to ascertain their possible interest in the proposal and to solicit comments, reactions, and suggestions to be taken into consideration in developing a complete proposal. It is advisable to check with the funding source to see if they prefer to receive such a brief prospectus. Otherwise, the best approach is to prepare the proposal in its entirety, including a summary, and to submit this to the funder.

A number of governmental funding agencies include a box on the first page of their grant applications to be used for the summary. Some federal funding agencies and foundation proposal reviewers prepare their own summaries to be used in screening proposals. By preparing his or her own summary, the applicant can stress whichever points are wanted. In addition to covering all aspects of what is included in the proposal, the summary should convey the way in which the proposal is responsive to the funder's requirements and interests.

There are different schools of thought among experienced proposal writers regarding a number of issues related to summaries. These include:

Inclusion of a summary in the covering letter

Inclusion of a summary in the Introduction section

Preparation of a separate summary section at the beginning of the proposal

Preparation of a separate summary section at the end of the proposal

Reference in the summary to the amount of money requested or omission of this aspect

More important than the resolution of these issues, however, is the quality of the summary itself. To capture the essence of the proposal, impress the funder, and to make the reader want to know the whole story are the important considerations.

Introductory Statements

The introduction to the proposal should include certain basic descriptive material, such as:

The title, with a short explanation of the proposed program

The name of the funding source

The name of the applicant

The RFP, legislation, program, or special interest (of the funder) to which the proposal responds

Introductory material should also cover the following substantive items:

The basic program concept or approach that is proposed

The nature and the scope of the problem

The geographic area where the program will take place

The persons who will be served

The importance or significance of the program

It is important to establish the central (or core) idea, theme, or concept that guides the proposed program. This programmatic concept should be logically linked to the way in which the problem is defined. Together, the problem definition and the program strategy represent the basic *theme*, which the rest of the proposal expands, clarifies, and defines.

The introductory part of the proposal can also be used to briefly describe the applying organization and enhance its credibility. Longer detailed descriptions of the organization, however, can be attached as a "capability statement," since such detail within the body of the proposal can be diversionary to the reader. Organizational credibility can be established by a variety of techniques: history, prior experience and successes, availability of supporting resources, support of cooperating groups, references to the organization's work or to the importance of the addressed problem to already credible groups (for example, commissions).

Some proposal writers believe that the introduction should focus mainly on describing the applicant's organization and establishing its credibility. As pointed out earlier, however, this can be distracting to the reader who wants to get to the substance of the proposal.

The introduction should clearly state which type of program is being proposed. It should give an indication of the nature and scope of the problem or need to be addressed, but the detailed presentation of the problem or need will come later. Similarly, a general statement of the program methods should be given, but the detailed program activities will follow.

The introduction should heighten the reader's curiosity, anticipation, and interest in reading on. Therefore, the introduction must be written interestingly and to the point. It is extremely important to be clear about all aspects of the proposed program. After the proposal is completed, it may be necessary to revise the introduction in order to eliminate any ambiguities or fuzziness that might have crept in during its initial drafting. Most proposal writers find that, as they are proceeding with the proposal, it is necessary to make revisions in former sections. This is a sign of good writing and one should not hesitate to do it.

A decision that must be made early in the proposal-writing process is the extent to which the proposal will be personalized or institutionalized. "Personalized" means the extent to which the form of the proposal uses personal references and the content is personalized. For example, one can begin a proposal being personal by saying,

"We are submitting this proposal to develop a new program for training drug-abuse counselors to you, based on the experience of Sam Jones and Mary Smith in similar activities in New York City."

Alternatively, the proposal can be institutionalized and begin,

"This is a proposal to develop a new program to train drug counselors based on pilot experiments in New York City."

It is more effective to institutionalize presentation and proposals and not to overpersonalize them. Identification of proposal concepts and methods with personal concepts and experiences tends to detract from the more general importance and applicability of the concept and program that is being proposed. This does not mean that a proposal should be devoid of reference to real people and real experience when this can be used to strengthen a particular aspect of the presentation. What it does mean is that the tone of the proposal is primarily professional, and organizationally oriented. It is not necessary for depersonalized writing to be duller or less interesting than personalized writing. On the contrary, it is not unusual for readers to simply skip over those sections of the proposal that relate personal experience.

There are many ways in which overly personalized presentations can be avoided. One should reduce the use of personal pronouns wherever possible. For example, instead of, "we propose," one can say, "*it* is proposed." Instead of saying, "it appeared *to us* that" one can say, "it appeared that." Instead of, "*our* objectives are" one can say, "*the* objectives are."

Each section of the proposal should set a framework or context for the section that follows. In addition to accomplishing this by a logical flow of ideas, it can also be furthered by using sentences at the end of each section that serve as a bridge to the next section.

This can be done in a variety of ways. An example is: "The next section of the proposal will go into more detail regarding its purpose and specific objectives."

Purpose and Objectives

A statement of broad overall purpose, mission, or goal and a listing of specific objectives is crucial to presenting a strong and clear proposal. This may be done as a part or subsection of the Introduction or in a separate section with its own title, "Purpose and Objectives." Both the *format* and the *substance* of the purpose-and-objectives section are important considerations in preparing a high-quality proposal. Both of these aspects are discussed in this chapter.

The *purpose* can usually be expressed in one or two paragraphs of narrative text. This is the most general or abstract statement made in the proposal regarding the expected achievements or benefits of the program. The purpose represents the broad goal of the proposed program or activities. It is not sufficient to say that the purpose or goal is to provide a service. A broad result or benefit of the service should be indicated. For example, neither "to provide family therapy" nor "to establish a neighborhood health center" is a purpose. However, by adding "in order to strengthen family life" or "to improve the level of individual, family, and community health," a proper expression of the program's purpose is achieved.

The *objectives,* on the other hand, require more specific statements of what will be accomplished. From the standpoint of format, the objectives are often better presented as a list than in paragraph form. For example:

The objectives are:

1. _____
2. _____
3. _____
4. _____
5. _____
6. _____

Most proposals seem to require from three to ten objectives, although it is not possible to establish a rule. To state objectives means to express program strategies in terms of what is expected to be accomplished. Objectives stand halfway between the general statement of purpose and the detailed explanation of program activities to be presented later in the proposal. Some proposal writers derive objectives from the purpose. Others set up their specific objectives and then generalize these into an overall purpose. Still others outline program activities and develop objectives to encompass these activities.

Taken together, the substance of the purpose and objectives should convey the benefits that will result from the program to individuals, families, groups, institutions, communities, and society in general, or to a particular field of knowledge. These benefits are usually intrinsic in the sense that they are well accepted as being worthwhile in their own right. For example, the objectives of a program to meet the needs of older people for social, recreational, and cultural activities might be to: *a.* reduce their social isolation, *b.* facilitate their feeling themselves part of the larger community, *c.* share their experiences with other groups in the community, *d.* reduce their dependency on other kinds of services, and *e.* contribute to their physical health and well-being. All of these are benefits not only to the older people themselves but to the community and the broader society. If these benefits are not conveyed in the purpose and objectives, then additional narrative text may be necessary to be sure that they are stated clearly.

In some government forms that are used to provide an outline of what must be covered in a proposal, objectives are referred to as "specific aims." Similarly, objectives as we have defined them may be referred to in some forms as "purposes" or "goals." Regardless of the nomenclature that is used, the general principles and approach suggested should be used to assure the clarity and consistency of the proposal and to contribute to the logical flow of the narrative.

Examples of objectives related to a program of counseling and group activities for single-parent families with a purpose such as "strengthening family life" might be:

1. To increase meaningful relationships among families with similar problems
2. To reduce isolation among single-parent families
3. To improve child-rearing skills
4. To facilitate the ability of families to identify the source of problems that concern them
5. To improve the ways in which families make decisions and allocate roles

Examples of objectives related to a neighborhood health center whose purpose is the "improvement of individual, family, and community health" might include:

1. To make preventive and primary care more accessible
2. To decrease the incidence of morbidity and mortality
3. To reduce environmental health hazards
4. To provide for continuity of care through the coordination of necessary health services
5. To reduce the extent to which hospitalization is required.

It should be stressed that all these objectives include words that explicitly indicate *action and a measurable result*, such as reduce, increase, decrease, make more accessible, or improve. Other active verbs used in expressing objectives include select, describe, demonstrate, formulate, identify, and recruit.

It is important to express objectives in specific, active, outcome-oriented terms. Such terms as help families, educate families, provide health care, or attack health hazards, even though they are active verbs, are not an equally effective way to phrase objectives, because they do not convey a sense of what the outcome will be.

The exact method by which each of the objectives will be accomplished should be described in the later section of the proposal on program activities or methods. Program methods (that is, the means or the way in which something will be done) must not be confused with program objectives (that is, the results or the ends of the program).

The statement of objectives is strengthened by phrases that define specific programmatic targets. For example, an objective "to improve the skills of reading teachers" can be strengthened by defining what kinds of skills are to be improved. Thus, the objective is strengthened by stating "to improve the *diagnostic and remedial* skills of reading specialists."

Similarly, programmatic targets expressed in terms of the characteristics of populations to be served can be included in objectives. For example, an objective "to raise the reading levels of children" can be improved by adding "to raise the reading levels of children in public-school grades one through four."

Many proposal writers and program planners believe that the best way to express outcomes is in terms of some behavioral change. That is, the outcome should be stated as a specific observable or measurable change in behavior or attitudes. It should be noted that this may be appropriate for the objectives for program and training proposals but that it may not be appropriate for research proposals, where the outcomes are expressed in the specific kinds of information, findings, and conclusions that will result from the research. But even in the case of research proposals, the objectives are strengthened by stating them in outcome-oriented active terms. For example, an objective of a study of hospital utilization may be "to determine the extent to which hospital beds are underutilized." This is a better statement than "to study the utilization of hospital beds," since it specifies that there will be an expected outcome, that is, a determination of the extent to which beds are underutilized. In Chapter 6 this aspect of research proposals is discussed in more detail.

Objectives should be stated in terms susceptible to a form of measurement. Therefore, they can provide the basis for designing an evaluation of the program as described on page 53. In this sense the objectives are also criteria for evaluation and assessing effectiveness.

Funders are putting increased emphasis on the importance of an adequate statement of objectives. This is due in part to the current popularity of various objective-oriented methods being used in program management, such as "Management By Objectives" (MBO) and various systems approaches as means for planning programs and assessing performance.[4]

The objectives should also be related to the way in which the problem and need are described and analyzed, which comes in another section of the proposal. If, for example, one objective in a family-therapy program is to "reduce isolation," a part of the needs section should discuss the problem of isolation as a factor that contributes to family breakdown and the weakening of family life. Similarly, the later section of the proposal on program activities must be sure to include activities that are directed toward decreasing isolation, such as the forming of support groups among families being served.

In some governmental funding programs the major objectives are actually predetermined by the funder and set forth in the program-application material. In such cases the objectives can be included in the proposal by directly quoting them for purposes of reference. Funder-stated objectives should never be used without such reference, for that might imply they have originated with the applicant. An example of this type of situation is presented in the application material of the U.S. Department of Health and Human Services for institutions seeking funds under a health careers program. This program lists the objectives as follows:

1. Identify, recruit and select individuals from disadvantaged backgrounds, as so determined, for education and training in a health profession (medicine, osteopathy, dentistry, veterinary medicine, optometry, podiatry, pharmacy, public health and other health training);

2. Facilitate the entry of those individuals into such a school;

3. Provide counseling or other services designed to assist those individuals to successfully complete their education at such a school;

4. Provide, for a period prior to the entry of such individuals into a regular course of education at such a school, preliminary education designed to assist them to successfully complete a regular course of education at such a school, or refer such individuals to institutions providing such preliminary education; and,

5. Publicize existing sources of financial aid available to persons enrolled in the education program of such a school or who are undertaking training necessary to qualify them to enroll in such a program.

---

[4] Discussion of the development of objectives can be found in Robert F. Mager, *Preparing Instructional Objectives,* 2nd edition (Belmont, Calif.: Fearon Publishers, Inc., 1975) and P. Malie, *Managing by Objectives* (New York: John Wiley and Sons, Inc., 1972).

In this case, the major requirement that the proposal must respond to is one of methodology to show exactly how the prescribed objectives will be implemented. In addition, in a case like this it is possible to respond by making the objectives in the proposal more specific. For example, the number of individuals who would be recruited in objective 1. might be indicated.

In other cases the application material is quite vague. For example, the application guidelines for one program states: "the purpose of this program is the creation of a broad artistic climate in the United States in which its indigenous musical arts will thrive with distinction through artistic, educational and archival programs." In this type of situation the proposal writers must develop their own specific objectives.

Some proposal writers suggest quantifying objectives whenever possible with statements such as "to reduce high school truancy by 30 percent." This practice is sometimes required by funders and is appropriate to some projects. However, it often is quite unrealistic and does not reflect the reality of the state of the art in the social and behavioral field.

Problem Definition and Need

This section may precede or follow the statement of objectives, depending on the logic and flow of the proposal. In this part the nature and extent of the problem that results in a need for the proposed program are explained and documented. Convincing reasons should be given, using logical argument and documented evidence, to establish the need. This section also provides an opportunity to demonstrate that the applicant understands and is thoroughly familiar with the field in which it is planned to operate the program. Thus, it has the added impact of helping to establish credibility and capability.

The general overall problem context for the proposal should be presented; however, one must be careful not to "oversell" the scope of the problem, but to limit oneself to those aspects that the program will address. In doing this, it is advisable to state the problem in a general way and then to go on to discuss each specific aspect or component of the problem relevant to the proposal. For example, the proposal may be focused on development of a new program in a mental health clinic, such as provision of a set of services to women who have been abused. The explanation of the problem might describe the general nature and growing extent of abuse and violence in the country. But, the proposal should concentrate the details of the needs section on the specific problem of only those women who are abused in the area served by the clinic.

If the definition of the nature of the problem and its possible causes is different from dominant definitions, this must be clearly spelled out by explaining in which respect it is different. As an example, assume that the proposal is directed toward prevention of juvenile delinquency and an explanation is given that delinquency is in large part the result of the limitations and unresponsiveness of socializing institutions such as the schools. Two things must be done. First, explain the ways in which schools contribute to the problem, what their limitations are, and the consequences of such limitations for young people. Second, recognize the accepted explanations of factors that contribute to delinquency, such as the family, and explain the reasons why this factor is not the focus of the proposal. After that, the implications of the school-oriented definition for the kind of program strategy, objectives, and activities that are proposed can be indicated. In effect, what this convincingly establishes is the overall conceptual frame of reference of the proposal and the premises and assumptions that guide the approach to the problem of delinquency.

Upon explanation of one's view of the problem and the factors that contribute to, or that are considered to be determinants of, or that have a causal relationship to the problem, the need for the program should be documented. There are four main ways to document need, namely, by: *a.* quantitative documentation, *b.* qualitative documentation, *c.* pointing out the limitations of existing programs, and, *d.* showing evidence of demand. These are explained below.

QUANTITATIVE DOCUMENTATION

Quantitative documentation refers to the use of statistical and other quantitative information. This material may be presented in either absolute or relative terms, or both.

Absolute statements would be, for example: "There are 20,000 single-parent families in the county"; or, "The number of unemployed youth in the community is 5,000"; or, "The juvenile delinquency rate is 4.5 per thousand."

Relative statements would be, for example: "One out of every ten families is a single-parent family"; or, "The proportion of single-parent families to regular families is higher in this county than in any other county in the state"; or, "The juvenile-delinquency rate is higher than the national rate of 3.7 per thousand."

Usually both absolute and relative data are used. The obvious criterion in selecting data is to present the information that is not only pertinent to the proposed program, but that at the same time establishes a clear need for the program. There can be, of course, a fine line between selection of data and distortion of data. Distortion should always be avoided, since proposal reviewers easily identify such situations. For example, the community in question may have a low unemployment rate. This can be pointed out and then it can be shown how over time, as communities get older and change, these rates tend to go up. Some examples of this should be given. These can then be used to argue in favor of establishing a prevention or training program now, in order to avoid a more serious problem in the future.

To show the relevant figures simple tables can be used. All tables should get a number and a title. Table titles should be descriptive of what the table presents and should refer to both the vertical and the horizontal material. A table may be set up as follows:

Table 1.

TARGET COMMUNITIES	Race (number)		Race (percent)	
	BLACK	WHITE	BLACK	WHITE
Springfield	1,000	1,000	50.0	50.0
Delmont	500	4,500	10.0	90.0
Middletown	2,500	500	83.0	17.0
Total	4,000	6,000	40.0	60.0

The title should read:

Table 1.
Number and Percent of People Living
in Target Communities by Race

Whenever a table is used, some reference should be made to it in the text of the proposal. Phrases such as "Table 1 indicates . . ." or, "as shown in Table 2 . . ." are examples of such references. One of the most frequent errors made by proposal writers is to put in tables or charts that are neither explained nor referred to in the text.

QUALITATIVE DOCUMENTATION

Qualitative documentation refers to the use of statements regarding the problem that are not based on numbers, but on logical connections that can be made between different factors or ideas. Examples of such statements would be: "Family life is weakened by the lack of communication among family members" or, "Juvenile delinquency is intimately connected with alienation of youth."

These relationships can then be expanded and references may be cited from literature, research, or empirical evidence to further support the ideas. In this way qualitative and quantitative material can be woven together and a convincing argument can be presented. The material presented earlier in this section of the proposal, in which the definition and nature of the problem were described, also contributes to the qualitative documentation of the need.

LIMITATIONS OF EXISTING PROGRAMS

In most cases, there are already some programs in the community in the field in which one is planning to operate. It is important to recognize this in the proposal and to criticize existing programs or to point out their limitations in order to further persuade the reader of the need for the proposed program. The program proposal has to point out why other agencies cannot meet this need and it has to stress in which way the proposed program differs from existing programs. Often previous studies, reports, and newspaper articles can serve as bases for the discussion of the limitations of existing programs.

Another technique in presenting the material in this section is to show how the proposed program builds on prior efforts by expanding or modifying them in order to enhance effectiveness.

In the case of research proposals, it is always necessary to make reference to prior research in the same field and to show how the proposed research is related to prior work by overcoming some of the limitations of that work, by extending prior research, or by further validating or testing the results of other research.

EVIDENCE OF DEMAND

Another way to document the need is to provide evidence of demand for the program if such evidence exists. Waiting lists, results of surveys, and results of community meetings can be used for this purpose. Also, statements from other agencies, government officials, and newspaper articles may reveal community concern for the problem and a demand for the proposed program.

The needs section of the proposal may require considerable research. Reference to studies, reports, and literature should be included to indicate sources and to also demonstrate familiarity with the field. This not only serves to strengthen the need section but it also enhances the funder's regard for the proposer's capability and competence.

RESOURCE MATERIAL

Resources to be used in preparing problems, needs, and rationale material include:

1. U.S. Government census reports, population surveys, and the *Statistical Abstract*
2. Reports of local and state planning agencies
3. Annual reports of relevant agencies
4. Surveys done by local and state planning agencies
5. Reports of special presidential commissions and task forces
6. General literature in the particular field
7. Reports of legislative committees and published testimony given at public hearings
8. Newspaper stories

Materials of this kind can be located in local and university libraries. The reference librarians will be able to help in locating appropriate documents. They are an excellent resource, and are generally underutilized. Chapter 7 will list additional resources. The use of charts and graphs, such as pie charts, bar charts, and line charts, can greatly enhance the presentation of quantitative data and add impact to this section.[5]

Frame of Reference or Rationale

This material may be in a separate section, or in the introduction, the needs section, or activities section. Material that should be covered includes the philosophy or perspective that guides the proposal, any

---

[5]For a guide to the use of these techniques, see Robert Lefferts, *Elements of Graphics: How to Prepare Charts and Graphs for Effective Reports* (New York: Harper & Row, Publishers, Inc., 1981).

assumptions that are being made, and the relevance and significance of the project. In a sense, this material conveys the thought behind the program to the funder. It strengthens any proposal.

Many program or training proposals present this material rather briefly in the introductory or in the needs section. However, it is an essential separate section of all research proposals, since it is necessary to set forth the theoretical framework for any piece of research as well as to explain all key concepts and the operational (that is, concrete, measurable, or empirical) definitions of each concept. This is explained further in Chapter 6.

An additional part of the material that can be included here is sometimes referred to as "state of the art" information. This is a synopsis of similar or related work done by others in the field addressed by the proposal. Preparation of state-of-the-art information requires a certain amount of research, because it should be documented by referring to literature, reports, and other source material. State-of-the-art type of information is appropriate to all types of proposals. It is focused mainly on a discussion of methodology, such as the state of the art with respect to counseling, training, planning, or research techniques.

Taken together the objectives, problem definition, needs, and rationale provide the concepts, the justification, and the legitimation for the program activities or methods for which support is being requested. These activities should be described in the next major section of the proposal.

Program Activities

This section of the proposal should describe in detail each of the specific activities or tasks that comprise the total proposed program and how they will be carried out (that is, what methods or procedures will be employed). Every major activity or task should be included. The section should have a title, such as "Activities," "Program," "Methods," "Project Design," "Operations," or some other descriptive phrase.

The activities should be consistent with the objectives. In effect, the program activities are a description of how the objectives will be implemented; they are the means or methods by which the objectives will be achieved. This section not only explains the program but it also gives the applicant an opportunity to demonstrate his or her expertise in program, training, planning, or research methodology to the funder.

Most programs include many different activities. It is helpful, from the standpoint of format, to group similar activities together. For example, if it is a new program for which a number of start-up activities are necessary, for instance, locating a facility, forming a board or committee, or recruiting staff and training staff, these activities can all be shown as a subsection under a heading such as "Preparatory Activities." Similarly, if a variety of educational programs such as forums, classes, and movies will be offered, these can all be grouped under a heading "Educational Activities." When activities are grouped in this way, it is essential to list and describe each specific activity under its appropriate subheading.

When the activities section is organized in this manner, it is usually possible to present the activities and the tasks or steps in a sequential manner. A partial example of the grouped activities format is shown below:

A. Planning and Preparatory Activities
  1. Staff Recruitment
  2. Staff Training
  3. Selection of Advisory Committee
  4. Obtaining and Equipment of Offices
B. Educational Programs
  1. Preparation of Drug-Abuse Manual
    a. Obtaining Material
    b. Production of Manual
    c. Distribution of Manual
  2. Organization and Implementation of Drug-Abuse Workshops
    a. Selection of Workshop Leaders
    b. Selection of Workshop Participants
    c. Organization of the Workshop
    d. Workshop Content
    e. Conduct of Workshops
    f. Workshop Format and Schedule
C. Counseling Program
  1. Intake Procedures
  2. Counseling Approaches
    a. Individual Counseling
    b. Peer-Group Counseling

There should be a full description of the activity under each of the headings and subheadings, including specific methods to be used, organization of the activity, and the characteristics and number of people to be served.

One of the frequent weaknesses in presenting this section of a proposal is the tendency to only describe *what* will be done, but not to describe *how* it will be done. For example, in proposing establishment of a mental-health clinic, one of the activities may be listed as being "intake" and the fact may be described that there will be an intake unit that will screen prospective applicants for service. This is a description of *what* will be done. The proposal is strengthened by describing *how* this screening will be carried out. This can be achieved by describing the criteria that will be used for eligibility, the manner in which the criteria will be used, the way in which the intake activities will be staffed, the efforts that will be made to explain the intake process to applicants, and the methods whereby people in the community will be made aware of the availability of the service.

In addition to explaining how each activity will be carried out, it is desirable to provide estimates of how many people will be served by each activity. This should be done wherever possible. Also, the characteristics of the people to be served can be explained, such as age, sex, and problems presented.

For some proposals it can be an effective presentational format to repeat, in this section, each of the objectives and then to describe under the objective each implementing program activity.

For example, in the case of a drug-abuse prevention program, the format might look as follows:

Objective A: To increase the availability of reliable information on the effects of the use of hard drugs to high-school students. Activities to implement this objective would include:

1. Preparation of a drug-information manual
2. Scheduling and carrying out discussion groups for all high-school students
3. Training a group of high-school students to serve as peer educational counselors

In using this format one must be sure to describe how each of these implementing activities would be organized and carried out.

For instance, under "preparation of a drug-information manual" each step or task involved should be described including:

a. the kind of information that would be included
b. the way in which the decision would be made regarding the information to be included
c. the sources where the information would be obtained
d. the methods by which the information would be obtained
e. the steps that would be taken in actual writing and producing the manual

   f.   the description of what its format would be

   g.   the manner in which the manual would be distributed and used

The foregoing format may not lend itself to proposals in which the same activity is an implementing device for more than one objective. Nevertheless, the same kind of step-by-step description of the activity should be used.

     Another way of relating activities to objectives is by using a simple chart that lists each objective on one axis and each major group of activities on the other axis. Wherever an activity directly implements an objective, a check is placed in the appropriate box. An example of such a chart is shown in Table 2.

Table 2.

Objectives	Activities			
	Counseling	*Education*	*Health Services*	*Referral*
Reduction of Truancy	X	X		
Improved Peer Relationships		X		X
Increased Understanding of Drug Abuse		X	X	

This will most likely be the longest section of the proposal. In the final analysis, the program activities are what the funder is really supporting; so they should be complete, specific, and task-oriented. If it has not been established in other parts of the proposal, this section of the proposal can also contain information on the reasons why particular program methods have been chosen and why these appear to be viable and effective. At the same time, reference can be made to any available evidence of effectiveness of similar program techniques. Also, the choice of certain methods can be linked to the particular characteristics or needs of those to be served. Some of the limitations of previous methods may be discussed.

     In addition to the narrative description of the proposed activities, it is also helpful to use charts to show the organization of activities and/or the flow of people through the program. An example of a simple chart is shown in Figure 4. A helpful tool that can be used in preparing charts and diagrams is a plastic template available from most office-supply stores. There are hundreds of types of templates. Some of the ones with the most useful sets of symbols, such as arrows, rectangles, triangles, and circles are the Pickett, Koh-I-Noor, and Besol computer diagrammers.

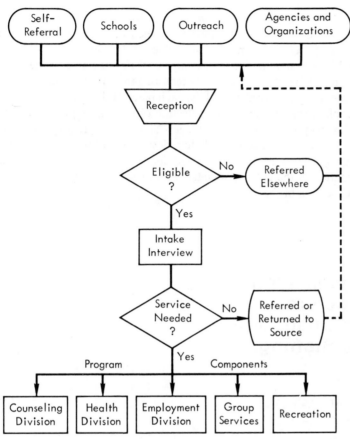

Figure 4.   Service Flow Chart; as an example, a multi-service youth program is shown.

FUTURE PLANS AND FINANCING

More and more funders are raising the question of future plans for programs that are initiated with special funds. These plans should be explained somewhere in the proposal—either in the activities section, in a separate section, in the letter of transmittal, or in the introduction. If the program will generate its own support through fees and contributions, this should be indicated. If after initial funding for one to three years it will become part of a larger ongoing operation, or if it will then be supported by another source, the plan for bringing this about should be specifically described.

FACILITIES

A description of physical facilities and program equipment should be included. This is especially important when proposed programs require special facilities or when a considerable part of the requested budget is needed for physical facilities or equipment. For example, if the proposed program includes a set of activities requiring the use of portable video-tape equipment, the proposal should list each piece of the necessary equipment and explain the reason for the selection of this particular type of equipment and its programmatic advantages. Similarly, a program for a halfway house for runaways should include a description of the location and kind of facility that would be used and its programmatic advantages. An explanation of the costs associated with these items should appear in the budget section of the proposal.

Organizational Structure, Administration, and Staffing

ORGANIZATION AND MANAGEMENT

Boards and committees should be described in terms of their membership, composition, and responsibilities. The manner in which they are appointed and their relationship to each other should also be pointed out.

Several other aspects of the organizational plan should also be explained. These include the locus for policy and program decision-making, the hierarchy of personnel, lines of communication, and arrangements to assure direction, coordination, and control of the project.

If the proposed program is part of a larger operation, an explanation is needed of the way in which the proposed program fits into the overall structure. If formal working relationships with other agencies are required, these linkages should be described.

Charts can be used to help clarify the organizational plan. A sample of a typical organizational chart is shown in Figure 5. This chart combines both administrative units (that is, boards and committees) and staff organization. It is also possible to use two charts: one showing administrative units, the other just the staff organization. The charts must be titled appropriately and be referred to in the text.

The sample organizational chart should be accompanied by a narrative that points out:

1. The board of directors, the size of the board, the persons on the board and the organizations that they represent, and the responsibilities of the board for policy making, fund raising, selection of personnel, establishment of personnel policies, and monitoring of the program.

2. The role, function, and responsibilities of each of the three committees shown on the chart, that is, the finance, personnel, and program committees.

3. The delineation of the responsibilities of the executive director, his or her relationship with the board and board committees, and his or her responsibilities for selection and supervision of the rest of the staff.

4. The description of the management responsibilities of the program director, the director of health services, and the director of social services. If these persons are supposed to meet as a staff planning group, for example, this kind of arrangement should be described and explained.

Figure 5. Organization Chart.

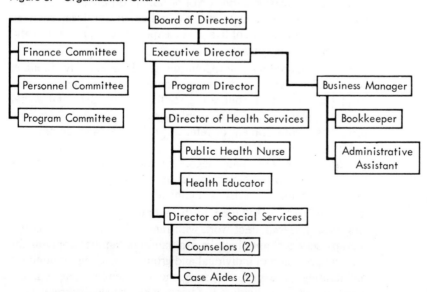

This section affords an opportunity to demonstrate administrative and managerial ability and know-how. It will give the reader confidence that the operation will be efficiently managed.

STAFFING

Each staff position should be listed with a brief description of responsibilities and qualifications. For each position the level of effort, that is, full time, half time, one hundred days, and so on, must be indicated. However, it is not necessary to show salaries here: they will be in the budget. In addition, the manner in which the staff is organized should be described in terms of lines of responsibility, unless this has been done in the prior section of the proposal. An organization chart can also be used for this purpose.

In some cases it may be expeditious and clearer to combine the material on staffing with the material from the previous section (on organizational structure) into a single major section with subsections.

An example of how to set up the staff descriptive list follows:

One Project Director, full time, twelve months.
Responsibilities: Overall planning, direction, coordination, management and supervision of the program; liaison with community agencies and organizations; management of fiscal affairs; interpretation of policies and procedures to the community; staffing board committees; supervision of program coordinators.
Qualifications: Graduate degree in human services, such as social work; minimum of five years' experience in program supervision and management.

One Program Coordinator for Counseling, full time, twelve months.
Responsibilities: Direction of all counseling and therapy activities; supervision of counseling staff (psychologists and social workers); planning and implementation of in-service staff-training programs; establishment of referral procedures with community agencies.
Qualifications: Graduate degree in human services, such as social work or psychology; minimum of three years' experience in provision and supervision of clinical services.

Two Social Workers, full time, twelve months.
Responsibilities: Direct work with families accepted for family-therapy services; initial intake evaluation of families applying for service; provision of individual and group counseling for families; maintaining case records; assignment of children to clinical psychologist for individual treatment when necessary; referral to

community agencies; participation in program-evaluation activities; participation in staff supervisory conferences.

Qualifications: Master's degree from accredited school of social work with specialization in counseling or case work; minimum of two years' experience in family therapy or counseling.

Two Clinical Psychologists, half time each, twelve months.

Responsibilities: Direct work with individual children accepted for treatment and with their families in individual and group-therapy sessions; establishing and implementing treatment plans for each client; administering psychological tests and evaluating client progress; referral to other agencies, maintaining case records; participation in program-evaluation activities; participation in staff supervisory conferences.

Qualifications: Advanced degree and certification in clinical psychology.

An alternative to the preceding narrative format is to use listings of responsibilities and qualifications. The listing would look like this:

One Project Director, full time, twelve months.

Responsibilities:

Overall planning, direction, coordination, management, and supervision of program

Liaison with community agencies and organizations

Management of fiscal affairs

Interpretation of policies and procedures to the community

Staffing board committees

Supervision of program coordinators

Qualifications:

Graduate degree in human services

Minimum of five years' experience in program supervision and management

Longer complete job specifications or descriptions for each position should be given in an appendix and referred to in this section. Similarly, if it is known which persons will fill various jobs, their names should be included in this section and their full résumés attached in an appendix.

In this part of the proposal any special aspects of the approach to staffing the proposed program that have not been covered earlier can be discussed as well. For example, if the program stresses the utilization of an interdisciplinary approach to providing services an explanation can be given here why this approach is being stressed and in which way the various staff responsibilities and qualifications serve to implement such an approach. If certain professional or experiential competencies among the staff are being stressed, an explanation of that approach can be given here and the manner in which the staffing pattern implements such an approach can be pointed out.

An example of how this can be done follows:

> As we stressed in the section of the proposal on program activities, the provision of effective counseling for older people is highly dependent on the special abilities of the counseling staff. This staff must be able to communicate effectively with older people, to relate constructively to this group, and to have the technical skills to locate and marshal the necessary housing, health, recreational, educational, cultural, and income-maintenance services they require. For these reasons, we have built these abilities into the job descriptions presented below as aspects of both the job responsibilities and job qualifications for each counseling position. Although we will employ staff without regard to any age qualifications, we are confident that the approach will result in a staff of primarily older persons who hold professional degrees in the counseling area.
>
> This approach to staffing the project is consistent with and contributes to the achievement of the program objectives (described earlier in the proposal) aimed at providing role models for older people in the delivery of human services. The following is a description of each position.

This kind of explanation, which should appear early in the staffing section of the proposal, not only sets forth the organization's approach with respect to staffing but ties this approach up to both the program's objectives and the specific job descriptions. This contributes to the internal consistency of the proposal; it is an indication of careful program planning on the part of the proposing organization.

Timing

To include a section on timing strengthens the proposal and supports the program and organizational plan. The section should explain how long the program will last and when each activity will begin and end. This can best be done by using a GANTT or MILESTONE chart as shown in Figure 6.

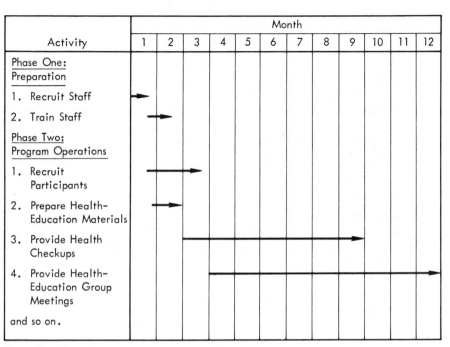

Activity	Month											
	1	2	3	4	5	6	7	8	9	10	11	12
Phase One: Preparation												
1. Recruit Staff												
2. Train Staff												
Phase Two: Program Operations												
1. Recruit Participants												
2. Prepare Health-Education Materials												
3. Provide Health Checkups												
4. Provide Health-Education Group Meetings												
and so on.												

Figure 6.   Timetable.

Each activity described in the program or methods section of the proposal should be listed on the left side, with a line and arrow showing the start and the end of the activity. This is a GANTT chart. If a triangle (△) is used instead of an arrow, it is usually referred to as a MILESTONE chart. In addition to the chart, a few paragraphs of narrative must be included summarizing the timetable. Aspects of the timetable that may not be clear from the chart, particularly the relationship between the timing for different activities, have to be explained. For example, if a month is needed to organize a board or committee before staff can be recruited, an explanation is needed why the staff recruiting does not begin until the second month. If there is an evaluation activity, the rationale for starting it at the particular time indicated in the chart must be given. This type of explanation makes the timetable clearer to the funder and it demonstrates the applicant's understanding of the intricacies of program management.

A degree of confusion exists about the terminology used by some funders in requiring a timetable. These funders may refer to the necessity of including a PERT chart in the proposal. PERT stands for "Program Evaluation Review Technique." It is a more complex, often computer-aided method for identifying the relationship and dependence over time among a wide variety of tasks. It was originally developed for use in construction projects. PERT is generally an inappropriate method for expressing timetables for relatively small service programs. When "PERT" is referred to, in reality often a very complete GANTT or MILESTONE presentation is meant. A PERT chart in its most simple form is shown in Figure 7.

In a PERT chart the numbered circles represent a sequence of events, such as:

1. Approval of grant
2. Approval of job descriptions
3. Hiring of staff
4. Training of staff
5. Beginning of program

The numbers in the event circles do not represent time; they are used simply to identify events.

The arrowed lines represent the necessary activities that connect these events. The events represent the start or completion of the activity. The numbers on the lines represent the time period (number of days) to progress from one event to the next.[6]

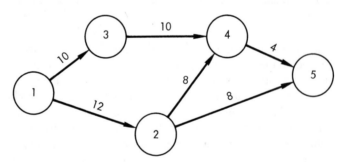

Figure 7. PERT Network.

---

[6]See, for example, Harry Evarts, *Introduction to PERT* (Boston: Allyn & Bacon, Inc., 1964).

Evaluation

If there is to be an evaluation as part of the proposed program, it should be described in a separate section that sets forth how it will be accomplished. Some proposal writers include this as a subsection under "Program Activities."

Funders vary as to their requirements for a formal evaluation of the program. If an evaluation is required or believed desirable, it often causes considerable consternation for proposal writers who are unfamiliar with research and evaluation techniques. It even troubles those who do know these techniques, because they recognize that *a.* the characteristics of many social programs are not susceptible to a conclusive evaluation of effectiveness; *b.* the requirements for reliable evaluation of social programs are quite complex; and *c.* the resources usually made available for a proper evaluation are inadequate for the requirements.

It is necessary to be clear about the primary purpose of the evaluation. Is it mainly to assess the effectiveness of program methods or approaches that are being demonstrated? Is it to provide funders with a basis for considering refunding or funding additional similar work? Is it to meet a legislative requirement? Is it to ascertain the effectiveness of one program approach compared to another type of approach aimed at the same problem? Is it to be used as a feedback mechanism, so that changes in program methods can be instituted while the project is still going on? Is is primarily intended as a mechanism to provide increased accountability to the funder? The answers to these questions will help determine the nature and extent of evaluative activities to be built into the proposal.

It is important to identify the *level* of evaluation that is required by a funder or, if not required, that one still wants to include as a component of the proposal. The term "evaluation" often means different things. Clarity about what is meant and expected is the first step in preparing the evaluation section.

Evaluation can range from complex experimental research to relatively simple reporting and program-accounting activities. To evaluate the impact of a human service program by comparing a group that is served with a similar group that is not served is quite a different problem from providing reports on the number and characteristics of people served each month. When program evaluation is a component of a program proposal, the trend is to focus the evaluation on assessing the extent to which objectives are being achieved. Therefore this approach is elaborated in the material that follows.

There are a number of different ways to approach the evaluation section of the proposal. One way is to demonstrate understanding of the complexity of evaluation, and of its significance and its limitations. Then it must be indicated that an evaluation will be built largely around measuring the degree of effectiveness in accomplishing the program objectives, and that a major preparatory activity during the first month or two after funding will be to prepare a complete evaluation design that will be submitted to the funding source.

In taking this approach it is essential to list the tasks that would be undertaken to produce such a complete design. These tasks include:

a. Defining each project objective in operational terms, susceptible to measurement

b. Developing the measurements that would be used as indicators of achievement of objectives and impact

c. Identifying variables that influence program performance and outcome

d. Specifying data requirements and identifying the source for each type of required data

e. Explaining the instruments that would be required and the method by which they would be developed and pretested

f. Describing the way in which the data would be obtained, that is, the data-collection methods

g. Discussing any sampling that would be done

h. Indicating the kinds of data analysis that would be undertaken

i. Describing the content of the final report

j. Describing the staffing and managing of the evaluation

k. Developing a timetable for the evaluation

It may be necessary to go beyond this and to indicate the substance of a more complete design in the proposal. This means including a description of the kinds of measurements and data that would be used to assess progress in accomplishing objectives. One would also need to outline the specific sources of such data and describe the kinds of methods and instruments (for instance, questionnaires, interview guides, and so on) that would be developed to collect the data. The way in which these instruments would be pretested must be explained.

It is advisable to try to retain a degree of flexibility in relation to the evaluation methods that are outlined in the proposal, unless one is very sure of the research techniques that will be used.

The use of both qualitative and quantitative measures should be stressed. For the first year of a program, it is wise to indicate that *progress* in achieving objectives will be assessed and measured rather than *ultimate* measures of effectiveness. This is appropriate, since most programs take more than one year to really prove themselves. It would be called *formative* evaluation (as contrasted to *summative* evaluation) in that it contributes to the refinement or modification of program methods during the course of the program. At the same time, however, the funder must be assured that there will be concrete measures of the progress that is being made.

It is a helpful technique in the presentation to list each objective and to indicate the type of data that will be assembled and the method by which the data will be obtained.

For example:

Objective One: to increase interagency coordination
   Evaluation Measures
      Quantitative data: Frequency of interagency meetings
      Qualitative data: Perceptions of agency executives regarding change in interagency working relationships and communication
   Data-Collection Methods
     1. Review and tabulation of minutes of meetings (Explanation of how this will be done.)
     2. Interviews with agency executives (Explanation of the way in which executives will be chosen—sampling if any—explanation of the way in which interviews will be conducted, and information regarding the interviewers.

If an evaluation section is indeed included, the staffing section of the proposal must definitely show which staff members are responsible for design and implementation of the evaluation. If consultants are to be used, this should be explained. All the costs must be shown in the budget.

It will strengthen the presentation to indicate that periodic (monthly or quarterly) progress reports will be prepared. The accountability aspects of the operation are thereby reinforced. Federal, state, and local governmental agencies that fund programs, as well as foundations, often have formal reporting requirements along these lines.

A useful evaluation not only focuses on the extent to which objectives are attained but also identifies the strengths and weaknesses of the operation so that the former can be maximized and the latter modified. Thus, in setting forth the plan or design for evaluation, this must be included in addition to the measurement of results related to achieving objectives.

Another trend in evaluation is to provide information on the cost of various program methods and to relate these costs to the effectiveness of these methods. This approach can be taken even further in the sense of attempting to estimate, in dollars, the benefits to clients or to the community that are derived from various programs. These dollar benefits can then be compared to costs. Cost-effectiveness and benefit–cost studies and analyses are quite complex research designs. The ability to generate reliable and valid cost and benefit data for human service programs is a problem that perplexes even the most sophisticated researchers. Nevertheless, an evaluation approach is strengthened if some data of this type are included. The simplest kind of data would be to estimate the total cost for each major set of program activities within the total program. One can also compute unit costs, that is, the cost for each person served. These kinds of data can then be related to information on the extent to which objectives are achieved.

A frequent approach to the evaluation problem is to use a "third party" or outside evaluator. This involves retaining one or more consultants, a consulting organization, or a university to design and carry out the evaluation. In such a case the evaluation design and estimated cost for evaluation may be prepared by the prospective outside evaluators and included as part of the total proposal.

The evaluation section should always explain how the information that is collected will be analyzed and reported. A general outline of the headings that can be expected in the final evaluation report may be included.

Given the latitude of possibilities of what might be included in the evaluation section, it is highly desirable to obtain some guidelines from the prospective funding source of its evaluation requirements and expectations. These are sometimes spelled out in RFPs, program announcements, or other written instructions from the funder. If they are not, a personal contact should be made to obtain more information.

In summary, a complete evaluation section is really a subproposal that contains the elements of a research proposal.

Budget

The budget is a representation of the program expressed in dollar amounts of estimated expenses and income. Many government funding agencies have their own forms that must be used in submitting the budget to them. Examples of some of these forms are included in this book. The sample format discussed below and the suggested methods for estimating costs will be useful in completing such forms as well as in preparing budgets for foundations. Most foundations do not prescribe a budget form to be filled out.

Funding agencies are concerned not only with the amount of money requested but also with the question whether the request is realistic and well justified. In addition, correct presentation of the budget is helpful in convincing funders of the proponent's managerial and administrative skills and capability. As with all other parts of the proposal, the more that can be learned about the rules and procedures followed by the funding agency, the more the proposal can be made responsive to the funding agency's requirements. The following format and sample budget corresponds to generally accepted approaches to the presentation of a budget.

In addition to the budget itself, one should attach budget-explanation notes or sheets to explain the basis upon which budget items that are not self-explanatory have been estimated. These explanatory notes should be on a separate sheet(s) headed "Budget Explanation."

One of the the most perplexing problems facing all proposal writers is the issue of "padding" the budget by requesting more than is needed. This is done on the assumption that funders cut almost all budget requests by some amount. Padding is not recommended, since funders can generally recognize this practice. A realistic budget that is optimistic in terms of the estimated expenditures is more desirable. Although it may be subject to some reduction, this type of request enhances the proposer's credibility with the funder.

On occasion, funders reduce a budget to a total amount that would really make it unrealistic or impossible for the applicant to carry out the program effectively. It is always tempting to accept even a drastically reduced grant rather than nothing, but experience has shown that this can be a mistake. It results only in problems later on in the project. Grant seekers must be willing to say "no" to unrealistic cuts. Funders will respect them for taking such a position. Done diplomatically, it can be a positive factor in their consideration of the next request.

One of the most important principles in preparing the budget is to be sure that it corresponds to the proposal's narrative material. The personnel budget must include all of the positions described in the "Staffing" section. One should never show a salary for a position not previously discussed. The budget should provide sufficient funds to implement all activities listed in the "Program Activity" section. For example, one should not put an item in the budget for publication costs unless the narrative indicated that one of the activities will be to publish a report, newsletter, or other type of publication.

The major aspects of all budgets are expenses (or costs), income, and in-kind (or donated) items. These are explained below.

EXPENSE BUDGET

The expense budget includes the following:

Personnel

The personnel category includes three separate items: *a.* all wages and salaries paid to full- and part-time staff considered regular employees, *b.* fringe benefits or employee benefits, *c.* payment to consultants, other nonregular employees, or contractors.

SALARIES

List each position, time devoted to program, annual salary rate, and budgeted amount. For example:

Salaries	Amount
One executive director, twelve months, full time @ 20,000 per annum	20,000
One nurse, twelve months, half time @15,000 per annum	7,500

The best way to estimate salaries is to find out the range paid for similar jobs within the organization and in other organizations. Salaries that are in the upper half of this range should be selected to indicate one's intention to attract high-quality people and to follow progressive personnel practices.

If salaries include a mid-year increase, this must be indicated in the budget-explanation notes. If funds are being requested for a one-year (twelve-months) period for a new program, it is doubtful that all the staff will start on the first day of the project. Therefore, the budgeted amount must be reduced accordingly. For example, a full-time counselor may be required at $15,000 a year, but it will not be possible to hire the person until the second month of operation. The annual rate must be shown after the position, but only eleven months of actual salary should be included in the expenditure-amount column.

FRINGE BENEFITS

Fringe benefits represent the expenses for social security, retirement plans, health insurance, unemployment compensation, disability insurance, and other similar costs paid by the program. Any costs paid by the employees themselves should not be included in this item. Fringe benefits are generally shown as a percentage of salaries, with a note explaining what is included. Most large organizations already have a computed fringe-benefit rate, ranging 15 to 30 percent of salaries. (Some proposal writers prefer to show in the budget each fringe item rather than to use a cumulative percentage. For example, an item such as social security taxes would appear under personnel.) Fringe benefits are not paid for services of contractors or consultants, since they are hired as private contractors on a per diem or unit-cost basis.

A sample budget-explanation note, explaining the fringe-benefit rate, might look like this (figures used are for purpose of illustration and do not represent current rates):

Fringe Benefits on Salaries and Wages

Social Security	6.0%
State Unemployment	2.0%
State Disability	0.2%
Workers' Compensation	0.3%
Employee Retirement Plan	6.0%
Group Health and Hospitalization	2.0%
Group Life Insurance	1.0%
Disability Insurance	0.3%
Dental Insurance	0.5%
TOTAL:	18.3%

CONSULTANTS

Each type of consultant, the rate of pay, and the number of workdays that are being budgeted must be listed as shown in the sample budget on page 62. Each consultant should have been described in the "Staffing" section of the proposal. It weakens the proposal to put in a budget amount for "consultation" without specifically describing it and justifying it in the narrative.

Some government agencies and foundations have specific policies regarding the use of consultants and the rate of reimbursement. This can be ascertained by asking the funding-agency staff for its written regulations regarding use of consultants and contract services.

Other Direct Expenses

The second major category of costs includes all "other direct expenses." These are costs other than personnel. Costs included are:

a. *Travel* by staff, consultants and, if necessary, by the program's board members and participants. The detail and justification for travel costs should be shown in the budget itself or in a budget-explanation note. Out-of-town or long-distance travel must be shown separate from local travel; mileage, car rentals, and air travel must appear as separate items under "travel." Some funders have recommended travel and subsistence rates that establish maximum amounts to be paid for mileage, meals, and lodging. These can be obtained by request.

b. *Subsistence or per diem*. This item represents the reimbursement to persons for hotel and meals. The budget should show the number of days to be reimbursed and the amount to be paid per day.

c. *Office supplies* (consumables) consist of stationery, mimeograph paper, duplicating supplies, pens, and the like.

d. *Program supplies* such as training materials, instructional material, training manuals, and similar items to be purchased should be shown as a separate item and explained in the notes.

e. *Equipment* represents desks, typewriters, copy machines, duplicators, and so on. Each item and its purchase or rental cost should be listed and the total shown in the expenditure column. Funders have varying policies with respect to the extent to which they will fund purchase or rental of equipment and these policies should be ascertained.

An example of a typical equipment explanation follows:

Equipment (purchase) $1,100
2 desks @ 300 each = 600
4 chairs @   50 each = 200
1 typewriter @ 300   = 300
Equipment (rental) 500
1 duplicator @ 400 = 400
1 typewriter @ 100 = 100

f. *Telephone* (communications) should show the monthly estimate, number of instruments, and total expenditures (see sample budget).

g. *Rent* (facilities) should show the cost of office-space rental (indicating the number of square feet and cost per foot) and the total annual expenditure (see sample budget). If remodeling or renovation costs are involved, these should be shown as well.

h. *Other expenditure items* should be listed individually. These include postage, printing of reports, agency memberships in other organizations, special insurance, purchase of publications, utilities (if not included in rent), and computer costs.

i. *Miscellaneous*. Some successful proposals include a miscellaneous item in the budget, but it is much better to show every specific item of expense. If this is done, a "miscellaneous" item should not be necessary. It should be avoided if possible. Leaving it out shows the funder that careful planning has gone into the budget estimate.

Indirect Expense

Indirect expense or overhead refers to the costs that are incurred by the larger agency within which the project occurs. If the proposed program is not part of a larger operation, it should not include any overhead items.

If a proposal is *a.* for a program to be carried out as part of a larger operation, and *b.* if the larger organization will provide certain adminis- trative services such as payroll, office space, equipment, and so on, it is appropriate to include such costs as part of the budget. These expenses are figured as a percentage of salaries. Large organizations usually have a standard rate used for this purpose that may range from 10 to 125 percent. If the organization already has government contracts, this rate has most likely already been negotiated with government auditors. If one will not have such costs, this item should not be included in the budget. If one does have such costs but does not want them reimbursed, they can be included as in-kind contributions to the proposed program. The sample budget gives an example of how to show in-kind contributions.

Table 3.
Sample Budget Format for Showing In-Kind Contributions

	FUNDS REQUESTED	IN-KIND, MATCHED, CONTRIBUTED, DONATED
Personnel		
Salaries		
Executive Director, half time @ 20,000 per annum	—	10,000
Assistant Director, full time		
12 months @18,000	18,000	—
And so on		
Totals		

Income

Some proposed programs may have sources of income as part of their operation from fees, expected contributions, and so on. If this is true, then the estimated income must be shown as part of the total budget and

subtracted from the expenses to reach a requested amount as shown in the
sample budget.

SAMPLE BUDGET

EXPENSES
Personnel
   Salaries

Executive Director 12 mos. @ 20,000 per annum	$20,000	
Program Director 9 mos. @ 16,000 per annum	12,000	
Counselor 12 mos. @ 14,000 per annum	14,000	
Secretary 6 mos. @ 8,000 per annum	4,000	
Total Salaries	50,000	
Fringe Benefits @ 25% of salaries of 50,000 (see budget-explanation note)	12,500	
Medical Consultant—10 days @ 100 per diem	1,000	
Total Personnel		63,500
Other Direct Expenses		
Office Rental 10,000 sq. ft. @ 1.00 per sq. ft.	10,000	
Telephone—3 apparatus @ 50 p.m. for 12 mos.	1,800	
Travel 5,000 mi. @ .20 = 1,000		
4 return trips N.Y.–D.C. @ 100 = 400	1,400	
Supplies (detail provided in budget-explanation note)	1,000	
Equipment (detail provided in budget-explanation note)	2,000	
(Plus other items of direct expense)	———	
Total Other Direct Expenses		16,200
Total Direct Expenses		79,700
Indirect Expense or Overhead (see note) @ 50% of Salaries of 50,000	25,000	
Total Expense		104,700
INCOME		
Fees (basis explained in budget-explanation note)	5,000	
Total Income		5,000
Request		99,700

SUMMARY

Total Expense	104,700
Less Income	5,000
Net Request	99,700

An example of the budget application form used by many federal agencies is shown in Figures 8A and 8B. This is a relatively simple line-by-line budget, which should be accompanied by explanatory notes.

Some agencies use more complicated forms. A sample of one of these follows the first example (see Figures 9A and 9B).

FUNCTIONAL OR PROGRAM BUDGETS

Sometimes a funder may request a functional or program budget in addition to the line-by-line budget illustrated in the preceding example. Note that Part III of the Federal form in Figure 8A requires such information. There are also times when it is advisable to prepare such a budget in order to clarify the relative costs of different aspects of a multi-function operation. A program or functional budget requires that the total expenditures be allocated to the major functions or program components.

The steps necessary to do this are:

First, prepare the line item budget.

Second, devise the major functional activities or program categories such as administration, intake, health education, community relations, counseling services, training, evaluation, information, and referral. In very complex programs a major program category can be further divided into subcategories. For example, counseling could be broken down into counseling youth, counseling adults, and counseling aging persons.

Third, estimate the appropriate proportion of each line item that can be appropriately allocated to each functional category. For example, an Associate Director at $20,000 a year might devote one-half time on administration, one-quarter time on community relations, and one-quarter time on health education. In such a case, one would allocate $10,000 to administration, $5,000 to community relations, and $5,000 to health education.

Fourth, add up the amounts that are allocated to each category.

Fifth, prepare a budget that shows all the categories and the total dollar cost for each category. Attach a budget explanation sheet describing the detailed description of how the total for each category was reached.

PART III – BUDGET INFORMATION

SECTION A – BUDGET SUMMARY

Grant Program, Function or Activity (a)	Federal Catalog No. (b)	Estimated Unobligated Funds		New or Revised Budget		
		Federal (c)	Non-Federal (d)	Federal (e)	Non-Federal (f)	Total (g)
1.		$	$	$	$	$
2.						
3.						
4.		$	$	$	$	$
5. TOTALS						

SECTION B – BUDGET CATEGORIES

6. Object Class Categories	Grant Program, Function or Activity				Total (5)
	(1)	(2)	(3)	(4)	
a. Personnel	$	$	$	$	$
b. Fringe Benefits					
c. Travel					
d. Equipment					
e. Supplies					
f. Contractual					
g. Construction					
h. Other					
i. Total Direct Charges					
j. Indirect Charges					
k. TOTALS	$	$	$	$	$
7. Program Income	$	$	$	$	$

HEW-608T

Figure 8A. Budget application form.

SECTION C – NON-FEDERAL RESOURCES

(a) Grant Program	(b) APPLICANT	(c) STATE	(d) OTHER SOURCES	(e) TOTALS
8.	$	$	$	$
9.				
10.				
11.				
12. TOTALS	$	$	$	$

SECTION D – FORECASTED CASH NEEDS

	Total for 1st Year	1st Quarter	2nd Quarter	3rd Quarter	4th Quarter
13. Federal	$	$	$	$	$
14. Non-Federal					
15. TOTAL	$	$	$	$	$

SECTION E – BUDGET ESTIMATES OF FEDERAL FUNDS NEEDED FOR BALANCE OF THE PROJECT

(a) Grant Program	FUTURE FUNDING PERIODS (YEARS)			
	(b) FIRST	(c) SECOND	(d) THIRD	(e) FOURTH
16.	$	$	$	$
17.				
18.				
19.				
20. TOTALS	$	$	$	$

SECTION F – OTHER BUDGET INFORMATION
(Attach additional Sheets If Necessary)

21. Direct Charges:

22. Indirect Charges:

23. Remarks:

HEW-608T

Figure 8B.   Budget application form (continued).

65

DETAILED BUDGET FOR FIRST 12-MONTH PERIOD

	FROM		THROUGH	

DESCRIPTION *(Itemize)*			TIME OR EFFORT %/HRS.	AMOUNT REQUESTED *(Omit cents)*		
PERSONNEL						
NAME		TITLE OF POSITION		SALARY	FRINGE BENEFITS	TOTAL
		PRINCIPAL INVESTIGATOR				

CONSULTANT COSTS _____

EQUIPMENT _____

SUPPLIES _____

TRAVEL	DOMESTIC	
	FOREIGN	

PATIENT COSTS *(See instructions)*

ALTERATIONS AND RENOVATIONS

OTHER EXPENSES *(Itemize)* _____

TOTAL DIRECT COST *(Enter on Page 1, Item 5)* ➤

INDIRECT COST *(See Instructions)*	_____ % S&W* _____ % TDC*	DATE OF DHEW AGREEMENT: ☐ WAIVED ☐ UNDER NEGOTIATION WITH:
	*IF THIS IS A SPECIAL RATE *(e.g. off-site)*, SO INDICATE.	

NIH 398 (FORMERLY PHS 398)
Rev. 1/73   PAGE 3

Figure 9A.   A more complex budget application form.

66

BUDGET ESTIMATES FOR ALL YEARS OF SUPPORT REQUESTED FROM PUBLIC HEALTH SERVICE
DIRECT COSTS ONLY (Omit Cents)

DESCRIPTION		1ST PERIOD (SAME AS DE-TAILED BUDGET)	ADDITIONAL YEARS SUPPORT REQUESTED (This application only)					
			2ND YEAR	3RD YEAR	4TH YEAR	5TH YEAR	6TH YEAR	7TH YEAR
PERSONNEL COSTS								
CONSULTANT COSTS (Include fees, travel, etc.)								
EQUIPMENT								
SUPPLIES								
TRAVEL	DOMESTIC							
	FOREIGN							
PATIENT COSTS								
ALTERATIONS AND RENOVATIONS								
OTHER EXPENSES								
TOTAL DIRECT COSTS								

TOTAL FOR ENTIRE PROPOSED PROJECT PERIOD (Enter on Page 1, Item 4) ⟶　$

REMARKS: *Justify all costs for the first year for which the need may not be obvious. For future years, justify equipment costs, as well as any significant increases in any other category. If a recurring annual increase in personnel costs is requested, give percentage. (Use continuation page if needed.)*

NIH 398 (FORMERLY PHS 398)
Rev. 1/73

Figure 9B.　More complex budget form (continued).

Capability Statements

As indicated in earlier sections, it is essential to convey to the funder that the organization has the capability to carry out the proposed program effectively and efficiently. In part, this is established by the quality of the proposal itself. It is also dealt with directly by providing descriptive capability material in the proposal about the abilities, competence, resources, personnel, experience, record of successful achievements, viability, reputation, and philosophy of the organization. Some of this material may have been presented briefly in the introductory section of the proposal. References to capability may also have been made in the proposed program description and in describing the project staff. However, in addition, and especially in the case of large-scale requests, a separate part of the proposal that contains an overall capability statement is advisable. This can take the form of a section of the proposal or of an attachment or appendix. If it is decided to include a capability section, the reader's attention should be called to it in the letter of transmittal or in the introduction to the proposal.

Typically, a capability section should cover the following:

Brief history of the organization; its reasons for starting; the time and place of its start; the source of funds; and the problem or need it seeks to address

Overall philosophy, mission and/or goals of the organization

Experience of the organization; significant programs and achievements

Organizational resources, including qualifications and background of staff; boards and committees; offices and equipment; ongoing administrative structure; mechanisms for financial and programmatic accountability

Evidence of credibility, adherence to standards and ongoing support, such as total size and budget; membership in national organizations; meeting incorporation, accreditation and/or standard-setting requirements; endorsements from officials and other organizations, agencies, and community groups, newspaper editorials or commendations; citations and reference to the organization's work in publications.

6

Research Proposals

This chapter describes the characteristics of research proposals and outlines methods for their preparation. It assumes that the proposal writer has an introductory working knowledge of the basic concepts and methods of social research including the fundamentals of design, measurement, and analysis of quantitative and qualitative data.

WHAT IS A RESEARCH PROPOSAL?

A research proposal is a specialized type of proposal to gain financial support in order to obtain and analyze information to describe and explain a particular problem, issue, subject, or question. Research proposals may be for basic research aimed at advancing knowledge. Or they may be for applied research to examine behavior, attitudes, policies, programs, materials, procedures, or processes. Such research may contribute to a better understanding of specific phenomena or may be used to provide guidance for making decisions about policies, programs, procedures, operations, and finances. The principles and techniques that are included in this chapter are focused primarily on applied research in fields such as health, mental health, social welfare, sociology, psychology, economics, history, the arts and humanities, education, community planning and the like. In these fields proposals may take a variety of forms, including:

Evaluations of programs and policies

Descriptive, analytic, and comparative studies of programs, organizations, materials, or methods

Surveys of population characteristics and public opinion

Case studies

Needs assessments

Investigations of a particular problem or phenomenon

Experiments and quasi-experiments

Demonstration and testing of research methods

Studies of costs, benefits, and effectiveness

Operations research

Historical analysis

Theory testing

Epidemiological studies

Dissertations and theses

Cross-sectional studies

Longitudinal studies

In part, many of these distinctions are semantic. A study of the extent to which a training/work program has resulted in reduced welfare costs may be an evaluation, an analytic study, a case study, a cost-benefit analysis, and a cross-sectional study simultaneously. In preparing research proposals one of the first steps is to identify the primary focus of the research methodology and use this as a basis for identifying what kind of research is being proposed. Since there are usually a number of choices, one should consider the kinds of research in which the potential funding sources have demonstrated an interest as a criterion to decide how to classify the proposed methodology.

MAKING RESEARCH PROPOSALS MORE EFFECTIVE

Research proposals are often subject to more intensive technical review than program proposals. This is especially true of proposals submitted to funders that have the support of research as their major focus, such as the

National Institutes of Health and the National Science Foundation, two of the major federal agencies that support considerable research. The various research and development sections of the units and bureaus of all the major federal departments, such as HHS, HUD, Commerce, Agriculture, and Interior, have also been increasing the intensity of their review of the research and development proposals that they support. The same has been true among the larger foundations.

Many federal agencies and many state agencies and foundations that support research through grants and contracts use technical panels of reviewers from their own staff and of outside experts to rate proposals that have been submitted. This means that the success of research proposals is highly dependent on the extent to which they adhere to certain expectations or protocols that have become traditionally accepted in the field of research over the years. At the same time, reviewers pay considerable attention to the extent to which new, innovative, and promising research approaches are incorporated into the proposal. One of the challenges that the proposal writer faces is to write the proposal so that it adequately demonstrates a familiarity with the traditional methodological expectations and also promises to break new ground.

Because of their specialized nature, research proposals must meet certain requirements that differ from program proposals. There are seven major requirements for research proposals to which funders can be expected to pay particular attention. These include the need to effectively:

1. describe the particular *problem* toward which the research is directed.
2. review and discuss the relevant *related research and literature* that is pertinent to the problem being studied.
3. explain the *significance* of the proposed research in terms of how it will further knowledge and contribute to the solution of a substantive, theoretical, methodological, policy, organizational, or programmatic problem.
4. define the *conceptual framework* for the proposed research, including the basic concepts that are involved, their relationships, and their concrete manifestations.
5. indicate the *specific research objectives* or questions that will be addressed or the specific hypotheses that will be tested.
6. specify in detail the *research approach, methods, and procedures* that will be used to obtain and analyze data.
7. show the *capability* to conduct and complete the proposed work.

In addition, the research proposal should meet all of the criteria set forth earlier in Chapter 4.

The special characteristics of research proposals require that they follow a somewhat different format from other proposals. Research proposals should include the following components:

Letter of Transmittal
Title Page
Table of Contents
Abstract or Summary
Introduction, Topic, and Purpose
Statement of the Problem
Significance of the Research
Review of the Literature and Related Research
Theoretical Base and Conceptual Framework
Hypothesis, Objectives, and/or Questions
Research Design, Methods, and Procedures
Work Plan and Timetable
Organizational and Administrative Structure
Personnel (Staffing)
Budget and Budget Explanation
Capability Statement
Supporting Documents

The order and the organization of this material may vary considerably according to the particular kind of research problem and the research, design, and complexity. Some examples of different outlines for research proposals are presented later in this chapter.

Experience has shown that three sections of the research proposal are especially critical, and weaknesses in these sections often contribute to the failure of many proposals. These are the sections on (1) design and research procedures, (2) problem description, and (3) personnel. A lack of clarity, completeness, and consistency, and the presence of technical flaws are the main difficulties that arise in these sections. There are several ways in which one can overcome such problems. First and foremost, be very sure that the proposal demonstrates a high level of technical research understanding and skill. Proposal writers should not hesitate to use consultants and seek advice of other persons in preparing the research design. One should examine other successful proposals and use reference books on research design as handy ways to check one's own work.

It is essential that the methods section explain both what will be done and fully describe how it will be done. One of the most difficult aspects of describing research methodology is to achieve a balance between the tendency to be too brief (listing the major procedures without explaining how they will be implemented) or being too detailed (presenting an array of ideas and the minutiae of technical procedures). To overcome this, it is helpful to break the methods section down into subsections, as will be outlined later in this chapter. Identify a central methodological approach. Don't try to cover every detailed procedure, but describe all major activities in a way that demonstrates their relevance to the study's objectives and establishes your technical competence. Discuss the limitations of the methodology and how expected methodological problems (for example, interviewer bias or low return rate from a mail questionnaire) will be minimized.

A convincing and clear exposition of the problem, its significance, and a review of related work are indispensable for the success of the research proposal. It is impossible to write an adequate problem section without having done considerable investigation of the subject beforehand. Selective completeness is the key to success in this section—that is, citations and the discussion of the literature (theories and other research) should be limited to those directly relevant to the research. A tour de force of the literature is not what funders are looking for. A fewer number of relevant citations and an astute discussion of their relevance to the proposed research can be more effective than a long bibliography. At the same time, be certain that all major relevant work is mentioned in order to demonstrate that you are thoroughly conversant with the area. Talking and consulting with other persons in the field and asking them to review the material can be of help in making sure this section is as strong as possible. They can inform you of other research, suggest related theoretical work, and call attention to inaccuracies or lack of clarity. Make use of that most valuable but often underutilized resource person, the reference librarian. Use the various computer searches available at libraries to locate related material. However, be cautious in citing material from these searches without firsthand examination of the work. The computer search programs tend to turn up a good deal of material that may use key words similar to yours, but may not really be related to your research project.

The main weaknesses in the staffing section that adversely affect a research proposal's chances of success are the lack of experience, training, or track record of the personnel conducting the research. The three principal ways to overcome this defect are to (1) be sure to fully describe the research capabilities of the personnel listed; (2) demonstrate one's research competence by making all other sections of the proposal as technically expert as possible; and (3) include research consultants who have impressive credentials as part-time members of the research staff, if necessary.

In the remainder of this chapter the various sections of the research proposal are outlined. A check list of the specific material that should be covered in each section is provided along with suggested techniques for improving the effectiveness of each section. It is suggested that the reader supplement this material with the guidelines set forth in Chapter 5.

LETTER OF TRANSMITTAL

A letter of transmittal should accompany a research proposal. This should be done even if the proposal is submitted on forms prescribed by the funding agency. A one- or two-page letter usually suffices unless you are using the letter as a mini-proposal or letter of inquiry (see Chapter 8). The letter should contain:

> the name of the organization and researchers (with their organizational title and affiliation) submitting the proposal
>
> the RFP, program announcement, or funder interest to which the proposal responds
>
> a brief statement of the overall research strategy that will be utilized
>
> the amount being requested
>
> an indication of the special experience or capability of the proposer to successfully carry out the research
>
> how long the project will take to complete
>
> willingness to discuss the proposal with the funder and consider modifications

The letter should put emphasis on succinct statements (two to four sentences each) of the problem, the significance of the research, and the overall research strategy, design, or approach. If the proposed research is based on prior research one has done, this should also be emphasized in the letter of transmittal.

TITLE PAGE

The title page for a research proposal follows the same format as program proposals shown on page 25. Special care should be taken in devising the title for a research proposal since it represents, in effect, a very brief summary of the proposal. Another reason titles are important is that the title words may be used to list the research in the various computerized abstract and search systems, such as the Smithsonian Science Information Exchange, that are used to identify research information. Therefore, the title should include words that are descriptive and relevant to the specific subject being studied.

The title page should include:

the title of the research

names and addresses of the submitting agency and names of principal investigators

date submitted

budget request total

Certain common errors in titling research proposals should be avoided. One is the tendency to make titles too global and imply that the research will provide the definitive answer to a major problem, when in effect it is directed toward only one aspect of the problem. For example, a title such as "A Study to Determine the Causes of Unemployment" promises something that has eluded most social and economic research. A more appropriate and descriptive title might be "A Study of Social Factors Associated with Unemployment of Urban Youth."

A second mistake in titling research proposals is the tendency toward unnecessary technical mystification. Remember that the majority of research projects in the social, behavioral, cultural, economic, and political fields will be reviewed by staff, reviewers, and panels that may include some persons who are not experts in the specific area of the proposal. In addition, funded proposals are often listed in foundation reports, or Federal agencies may report them to members of Congress. It is no great honor to be selected for an award for an obtuse or overly grandiose title. Avoid jargon and ambiguity in the title. Avoid provoking unnecessary political sensitivity.

Follow the title page with a table of contents listing each heading and page number as described earlier on page 27.

ABSTRACT

The summary of a research proposal is called an Abstract. This summary statement may be 150 to 500 words. Most federal agencies require 200 or 250 words. The ideal summary is about one typewritten page, double spaced. Although the abstract appears at the beginning of the proposal it is usually the last part to be written.

It should include brief statements and paraphrases of only the most salient aspects of the proposal related to:

the problem and its significance

the purpose and objectives or hypotheses

reference to the major prior research

the overall research approach (such as case study, experiment, comparative study, and so on) its scope (what or who will be studied)

the major procedural emphasis (interviews, field observations, questionnaires) and the analytical approach that will be used

expected outcomes

When writing the abstract, include some of the key words used in the proposal narrative to sensitize the reader to the most important themes. Do the abstract carefully since it is usually the first part that is read; sometimes it is the only part read by some reviewers. In addition, the abstract (along with the title) may be used in the various national computerized information systems, so major reference terms should appear in the abstract.

Abstracts are difficult for proposal writers to prepare. They are so close to and involved with all of the material in the proposal that it is hard to select out only the key material. One way to overcome this problem is to time the writing of the proposal so that it can be put aside for a day or two before writing the abstract. Most writers start with abstracts that are too long. Combining sentences, omitting unnecessary qualifying words, and simply deleting entire sentences are ways to cut down on the length.

INTRODUCTION AND PURPOSE

The first part of the narrative is the introductory material. Some proposal writers omit this section since it may duplicate the abstract or letter of transmittal. In this case they start with the statement of the problem. If you decide you want a general introduction, begin with a few sentences that indicate what the proposal is about, its overall purpose, and the RFP number or specific program or interest of the funder to which the proposal is a response. Briefly summarize the essence of the problem and the research objectives and approach that will be used. In the case of research proposals the statement of purpose can be quite short and descriptive, such as "to conduct an evaluation of outpatient clinics" or "to examine the determinants of cost overruns among training programs." Such descriptive statements of purpose can be improved by adding an overall outcome, such as ". . . to determine the impact of their services . . ." or ". . . to devise cost-control mechanisms . . ." Mention any prior research you have conducted that represents a precursor to the proposed study. Finally, explain how the remainder of the proposal is organized.

Some proposal writers prefer to use most of the introduction to explain the capability of the researchers and their institution in some detail. The introduction is also a good place to point out how the proposal is directly related to other work funded by the grant program to which one is applying. Funders are attracted to efforts that represent continuity or an extension of successful projects they have funded in the past. If the prior work was unsuccessful or wasteful, it is important to differentiate the proposed research from that done earlier by other investigators.

THE PROBLEM AND ITS SIGNIFICANCE

The research proposal should focus upon one main topic of study, such as juvenile delinquency, stress, sleep, divorce, hospital costs, effectiveness of therapy, unemployment, effects of student-teacher ratios, and the like. Start this section of the proposal by describing and elaborating the main topic. The topic should be discussed as a research problem in the sense that there are unanswered or elusive questions about the topic and a need for more description, information, experimentation, or analysis. Then go on to describe the particular factors that are associated with the topic and that will be the subject of the research. The problem section of the research proposal is similar to the needs section of other types of proposals as described in Chapter 5.

The problem statement should cover three main interrelated points which may be all discussed in one section of the proposal, as separate subsections, or as individual sections with their own headings. The organization of this material will depend on the nature of the problem and one's writing style. The most important thing is to be sure that all three points are covered, presented in clear language, well documented, and responsive to the requirements of the RFP or the interests of the funder. The points are:

> the nature or characteristics of the problem, including what is known about it, and the conception of the problem that is being used in the proposal
>
> the extent of the problem and why the problem is or should be of interest and importance
>
> the usefulness of gaining additional knowledge related to the problem

The following are some guidelines to help present each of these points more effectively.

THE NATURE OR CHARACTERISTICS OF THE PROBLEM

An explanation of the nature of the problem is a way of defining the topic to make it susceptible to research. It is the beginning of developing the study's conceptual framework. The key to doing this is to identify and explain the relationship, influence, or effects of certain other factors (or variables) on the problem. For example, in explaining a topic such as student achievement in school, one might define it in terms of the effects of class size, student-teacher ratios, socioeconomic class, school facilities, and so forth. Or one might examine it in terms of textbook selection, library facilities, teacher qualifications, and such. In this way the topic is translated into a problem about which there is a need to determine the relationship or influence of these factors (variables) on certain outcomes, situations, or behaviors. Use the literature to document the factors and relationships you choose to include in the research.

THE EXTENT OF THE PROBLEM
The problem can be further elaborated by providing quantitative and/or qualitative information on its scope and extent. The number, distribution, rate, and trends in school dropouts, street crime, divorce, stress-related illnesses, or youth unemployment are examples of the kinds of data that can be used to elaborate the problem definition. Using these kinds of data also serves to highlight the importance of the problem and, by extension, the importance of the proposed research.

In addition to describing the extent of the problem, it helps to document a professional and/or public interest in the problem. This can be accomplished by referring to other research, journal articles, commission reports, legislative mandates, newspaper articles, and similar material. Pointing out the effects and costs of the problem to individuals, the economy, the government, the society, and institutions is an additional way to emphasize its importance.

USEFULNESS AND APPLIED VALUE
Because proposal writers and researchers are so very convinced of the importance of what they are doing, they often have a tendency to assume that the value of the research being proposed is self-evident. This is an error. It is necessary to be explicit about the significance of the proposed research by explaining in what ways it will contribute to a further understanding of the problem. One should specify how the outcomes of the research can be of applied value in the design of methods, material, policies, programs, or operations. Including this kind of information also prepares the reader for the later discussion of the specific research objectives or hypotheses.

REVIEW OF THE LITERATURE

Additional knowledge about the understanding of social problems takes place primarily as the result of either an extension of prior work or a criticism of prior ideas and approaches. It is important, therefore, to pay considerable attention to the section of the proposal that reviews the theories and the prior research and work that are related to the problem under study. This discussion can be enhanced by approaching the review of the literature not as a perfunctory obligation to the norms or research, but as a way of emphasizing the importance of the proposed research, adding richness to the problem discussion, identifying the state of the art, and helping justify the later description of the research design.

Following a few guidelines can enhance the effectiveness of this section. These include:

Be thorough but relevant—cover all of the major work, but do not attach long bibliographies of every possible citation.

Group the related literature—use categories built around different types of theories and different methodological approaches; or group it in terms of the key variables or concepts that will appear in the design.

Be critical and fair—discuss related work in terms of its strengths and weaknesses and point out the basis for these conclusions.

Illustrate how the proposed study builds on the prior work by replicating, extending, modifying, or challenging it through an alternative approach.

Depending on the flow of the narrative, one may also develop the study's conceptual framework here by describing each of the key concepts that are part of the study if those concepts are based on the literature being reviewed.

OBJECTIVES OR HYPOTHESES

There should be a separate section of the proposal that states the specific objectives of the study, the hypotheses to be tested, or the questions to be answered or addressed. Any or all of these may be addressed, and the section may be located either before or after the explanation of the problem and the literature review. It should precede the design, procedures, or methods section of the proposal.

Hypotheses are always stated in terms of expected or predicted relationships among variables that will be tested—for example: "Stress levels will be significantly greater for executives than for assembly line workers." Hypotheses must be linked to and supported by the theoretical and empirical knowledge base discussed in the section that reviews the related literature and defines key concepts. Formal hypotheses are most appropriate in studies where they can be subjected to statistical tests of significance. Hypotheses are, in effect, statements of the expected knowledge that will be an outcome of the study. It is seldom necessary to include null hypotheses in the proposal (even though they may be used in the analysis).

Objectives, on the other hand, are less formal outcome statements that do not speculate about the specific character of the expected relationships or findings. Instead, objectives are statements about what the research will achieve. An example would be: "The study will ascertain the extent to which the training program is reaching low-income persons" or "The study will identify the distribution of stress among executives and assembly-line workers."

In some cases neither the specification of hypotheses or objectives may be appropriate. In such cases one should at least state the questions that will be answered. For example:

> The study will address the following questions: Are schools adhering to Federal guidelines? Who are the principal school officials involved in policy decisions? Etc.

It should be apparent from the foregoing examples that as one moves from hypothesis to objectives to questions, the definition of a study's final outcomes becomes less precise. Thus, one should rely on the question format only in the case of studies that are of an exploratory nature and where it is not possible or desirable to be too specific about key variables. Otherwise, always use objectives unless hypotheses are called for by the design. Proposal writers frequently fail to recognize the ease with which questions can be converted to objectives. For example, a question such as "Were the classroom materials used suitably?" can be restated as an objective: "To determine the extent to which suitable materials were used in the classroom." Except in the case of exploratory studies, one should always use a statement of specific objectives in the proposal. If it is an experimental or quasi-experimental design using quantitative measures, the proposal should include formal hypotheses. Any good research text describes the characteristics and rules for the statement of hypotheses.

When stating the objectives of a research project present them in list form. They should meet the criteria outlined in Chapter 4. In addition to objectives that state what the study will substantively achieve (e.g., "determine the cost of the program"), there should also be one or more objectives regarding the report of the study and its dissemination. This is usually at the end of a list of objectives. An example would be:

> 8. To prepare a final report of procedures, findings, and conclusions and recommendation for submission to the Foundation and to agencies in the field.

If conferences or workshops are to be held or other devices for dissemination to be used, these should also be indicated as one of the objectives.

When stating objectives, always use active words and state them as outcomes of the research; for example, "to determine the extent of duplication among programs" is better than "to examine duplication among programs." Only include objectives that are related to points made in the discussion of the problem. Only include objectives that are feasible within the resources, time, and data base that will be obtained as outlined in the section of the proposal on design and procedures. Gear the presentation of objectives to the potential applied contribution of the study to the interests of the funding source. For example, if a funding program has a stated interest in "urban problems," include reference to "urban problems" in the discussion of the objectives.

RESEARCH DESIGN AND PROCEDURES

In practice, the term "research design" is used in a variety of ways. It is sometimes used to refer to the entire proposal, sometimes to research procedures, sometimes to the type of design (e.g., experimental design). Similarly, research procedures and research methods are used in different ways and sometimes are used interchangeably.

There are many different ways to organize and present the material to describe the research approach and methods that will be employed. A good deal depends on the nature and complexity of the problem and of the design. Regardless of how one organizes this material, there are six specific elements that should be presented, including:

a description of the type of overall design to be used and why it has been adopted

definitions of concepts and how they will be put into effect.

delineation of the variables or data categories, how they will be controlled, and what their relationships are

a description of the data sources, including populations or other units to be studied and how the sources will be selected

a description of the data that will be collected and the methods and procedures that will be applied

a plan for analyzing the data and their presentation

Each of these elements is discussed in the remainder of this chapter.

Overall Design

There is a wide variety of choices of overall design for social research. The proposal is improved by clearly stating the type of study approach being proposed, its general characteristics, why it is appropriate, its feasibility, and its limitations.

Research designs may be categorized in a number of ways. One way is based on the extent to which causal or associated relationships are or are not identified. Studies in which relatively little is known ahead of time about the variables involved are exploratory or formulative studies. As one can be more specific in the design with respect to variables, the study may be called a descriptive, analytic, or evaluative study. As the degree of control over variables increases, the design may be referred to as experimental or quasi-experimental.

Study designs may also be characterized by other methodological approaches. That is, whether they are case studies, experiments, comparative, longitudinal, cross-sectional, participant observer, sample surveys, among others. The overall research approach should be given a label, such as "a descriptive-analytic study of . . ." or "an evaluation of . . ." It should be described and discussed in terms of why it has been selected, its appropriateness and feasibility in connection with achieving the objectives of the study.

All researchers would like to obtain results that are as conclusive as possible. Some proposal reviewers may begin with this mindset and the assumption that the "pure" experimental design is the sought-for ideal, since it supposedly offers the most control over variables. This seems to be true, even though there is abundant literature of the weaknesses, to say nothing of the lack of feasibility, of the experimental approach in applied studies of social, economic, and political phenomena. To overcome this possibility, it is important to be specific about the way in which the selected research approach will produce the kind of data and analyses required to realize the objectives of the study. In explaining why the approach is appropriate, also make reference to the literature and other studies and to the state of the art. This can help to further legitimate the choice of design.

Explicate Variables

The design section is strengthened by a detailed discussion of the variables that will be studied and how they will be put into effect. A variable is a general class or category of objects, processes, structures, events, information, behaviors, or characteristics. As such, it is an abstraction. Each of the variables to be studied should be specified, and the empirical or observable characteristics (that is, the operational definitions) that will be used to represent the variable should be delineated.

There is always a good deal of latitude in operationalizing variables. For example, a variable such as "health professionals" might be defined as persons holding a degree in medicine, nursing, dentistry, or allied health. It could be further defined as persons working in health agencies (hospitals, clinics) who hold such a degree. In developing an operational definition, be sure that it is directly relevant to the way the problem has been defined and the way the objectives (or hypotheses) have been stated. Research proposals often are faulted for a lack of internal consistency, and it behooves any proposal writer to take great care that the material in this section of the proposal is consistent with the other sections.

In discussing variables it is productive to group them into appropriate categories, such as "dependent, independent, and intervening variables," or "input and output variables," or "benefit and cost variables" or "family, individual, and community variables," or whatever other general

Figure 10. Factor relationship chart. From *Elements of Graphics*, © 1981 by Robert Lefferts. Reprinted by permission of Harper & Row, Publishers, Inc.

categories may best suit the overall design. Make use of these categories as subheadings in the narrative description of the variables.

The expected relationships among variables should also be described and the way the study will ascertain the extent of these relationships should be briefly mentioned here, even though this will be discussed in more detail later in the data analysis section of the proposal.

The discussion of variables and their relationships is, in effect, the presentation of a conceptual and operational model of the problem or phenomena being researched. One can supplement the narrative with a graphic illustration of this material as a summary and in order to add clarity and impact. An example of this is shown in Figure 10.

Scope, Units of Analysis, And Data Sources

The explanation of the study design should include a description of exactly what the units (or subjects) will be studied, how they will be selected, how many will be studied, and where they are located. This material, along with the later discussion of what data will be collected, serves to clarify the scope of the study.

Indicate whether the primary units to be studied are individuals, groups, organizations, activities, policies, materials, books, and so on. The characteristics of these units should be described further by factors such as their demography (age, sex, etc.), geography (location), time, or other factors. It is surprising how frequently proposal writers fail to specify this rather fundamental aspect of a study, thinking it is self-evident.

How the units to be studied will be selected should be described in detail. In a study of individual opinion or behavior, it is often necessary to sample populations. In these cases, outline the sampling methodology and indicate whether it will be a probability sample involving randomization or a non-probability sample (such as snowball, judgmental, quota, exemplary cases). Include each step in the selection process and any statistical devices that will be used in selecting random samples. If samples are other than random, the steps in the selection process should still be explained. If organizations or programs are to be studied, specify what units, departments, offices, or activities will be examined and how and why these will be selected.

Data Base, Measurement, And Instrumentation

The 'design should specify how each variable will be measured through the use of tests, instruments, interviews, field observations, or other methods. If ratings, indices, and scoring devices are used, these should be explained. This section should describe how the variables (i.e., what is to be measured) will be represented by specific sets of data. If tests, interview guides, and questionnaires are to be used, the data items included in the instrument should be outlined. If, at the time of writing the proposal, the instrument is not yet developed, describe the step-by-step procedure that will be used to devise and pretest the instrument. In such cases indicate at least the categories or types of data that will be sought. Be sure these are explained in a way consistent with the definitions of the concepts and variables involved in the study and are explicitly linked to the study's objectives.

The validity, reliability, relevance, and sensitivity issues involved in each measuring device should be discussed. While social research measurement devices may not fully meet these criteria, it is valuable to demonstrate to the funder your awareness of the issues and limitations of these measures and of the extent of error that can be expected.

Data Collection Procedures

Having described the kinds of data to be collected, the next step is to describe the step-by-step procedures that will be employed to collect the data. This provides the reader with a picture of what the researchers will actually be doing. Depending on the particular type of study some examples of the material to cover here include:

How tests will be administered.

What kinds of interviews will be held, what procedures interviewers will use, how appointments will be made, how respondent cooperation will be assured, how interviews will be recorded.

What books, records, files, or documents will be reviewed, how they will be obtained, how data will be extracted from them and by whom.

What procedures will be used in making field observations, how they will be recorded, who will conduct them.

How mail questionnaires will be sent out, what devices will be used for follow-up.

How will data be filed, what control mechanisms will be used, how errors and inconsistencies will be identified and corrected, what methods will be used to assure quality of data.

What supervisory methods will be used.

The adequacy of the description of the research process demonstrates to the funder that the researchers know what tasks are involved and know how to do the work. It also documents the feasibility of the study and of the proposer's capability to successfully complete the project. It is especially important for new researchers without an established track record to provide a careful and complete presentation of this material. One should also check over this part of the proposal to be certain that it shows how expected obstacles (e.g., interviewer bias, failure to return mail, questionnaires, lack of cooperation, unavailability of records) will be overcome.

In the case of studies that involve a considerable range of data and a number of different data sources, the use of a graphic data matrix can be an effective technique. The matrix can show (a) major data items and (b) major data sources. The use of the matrix technique serves a number of purposes. It provides the reader with a well-organized summary of the design. It also contributes to the coherency, internal consistency, and impact of the proposal.

Data Analysis

One of the major factors that can affect the success or failure of a proposal is the adequacy of the plan for analysis and interpretation of the data. This section of the proposal should cover a number of the following items:

How data will be assembled, coded, processed, edited, filed, and collated.

What use of computers or other hardware will be involved.

How data will be categorized and aggregated.

What statistical methods will be used to obtain descriptive and inferential data and to identify relationships among variables.

What kinds of charts and graphs will be used: pie charts, bar charts, line charts, scattergrams (includes dummy tables and charts that are expected to result from the analysis).

What will be the basis for the interpretation of the data and/or hypothesis testing.

How the data analysis will be related back to the study objectives.

What step-by-step tasks and procedures will be employed in the data analysis phase of the study.

Final Report

Include an outline of the organization of the final research report in the proposal. The more specific the outline, the more the proposal will be strengthened. At a minimum all research reports should cover the following major topics:

A. An Abstract
B. Introduction
C. Problem Statement
D. Study Procedures
E. Findings and Conclusions
F. Appendices

This basic outline can be expanded by adding as many subheadings as possible. While these will depend largely on the particular problem and research methodology, there are a number of general areas that can be anticipated, as shown in the following outline:

A. Abstract or Summary of Method, Findings, and Conclusions
B. Introduction
  1. Purpose of the Study
  2. Study Objectives or Hypotheses
  3. Overall Research Approach
  4. Organization of the Report
C. Problem Statement
  1. Nature and Extent of the Problem
  2. Significance
  3. Conceptual Model and Definitions
  4. Related Literature Review
D. Research Design
  1. Overall Design
  2. Discussion of Variables and Operational Definitions
  3. Description of Data Sources
  4. Data Collection Methods
    a. Instrumentation
    b. Procedures
  5. Data Analysis Techniques
E. Findings and Conclusions
  Outline the major areas of findings that are expected to emerge and the areas in which conclusions will be presented. Use the problem definition, specific questions, objectives, or hypothesis described earlier in the proposal as guides to identify these specific areas in this part of the proposal. Include dummy tables and charts expected to be included in final report.
F. Appendices
  1. Sample Instruments
  2. Tables
  3. Other Background Information

WORK PLAN, PHASING AND TIMETABLES

A step-by-step work plan and time schedule should be projected and described in the proposal. Each operation or task should be listed in as sequential a form as possible, including the starting and completion time for each activity. Use one of the charts or diagrams explained on page 50 in Chapter 5 to make this section as clear as possible. In the case of federally funded projects where OMB approval of instruments is required, include the anticipated time for this procedure. In addition, some agencies require that instruments and/or statements of the more detailed design be submitted to them for approval before the next phase of the study can begin. Show these steps in the work plan and timetable as well. If a period of time for review and approval by human subjects review committees is required, show this in the timetable. A recognition of these kinds of possible delays contributes to a more realistic work plan and to the credibility of the proposal writer's research expertise.

Be particularly careful in scheduling time for data collection activities, since these tasks are most frequently underestimated in planning research projects. Every procedure described in the earlier sections of the proposal must be accounted for in the work plan and timetables.

In complex projects, clarity can be added by grouping the tasks into three to five major phases of the study, such as those illustrated in the sample chart in Figure 4 in Chapter 5.

ORGANIZATION AND PERSONNEL

As noted earlier, one of the major reasons for the failure of research proposals is that the reviewers are critical of either the qualifications of the proposed research staff or the organization of the staff. Experienced and established researchers, of course, do not have serious problems in this connection, but many proposal writers do not have a major record of performance. Thus, the way this section of the proposal is presented can greatly strengthen the overall chances of success. One technique is to list each position. Begin with the project director or principal investigator followed by the rest of the staff positions. Briefly describe the job responsibilities and qualifications for each. Where it is known, briefly describe the competency (name, experience, and training) of the specific person who will be in the major positions. Attach a vitae as an appendix to the proposal for each person in a key position. Rather than use routine file vitaes, it is better to prepare individual vitaes geared to the specific purposes of the proposal, so that the most relevant experience and training can be emphasized. In some cases, one may not have names of persons for all jobs. This is acceptable as long as the director/principal investigator and some top persons can be identified. Do not, however, include a specific individual's name and say "will be recruited if the project is funded." Make these arrangements before the proposal is submitted, or leave out the name.

Researchers without a track record can improve this section by including experienced persons as consultants and by stressing the overall research capability of the sponsoring institution or organization. When including consultants, be specific about their role and the tasks they will perform.

Explain how the staff will be structured and include an organizational chart as illustrated in Figure 5, showing lines of authority, communication, and supervision. Also indicate how the research unit will be related to the sponsoring institution. If committees or advisory groups are part of the plan, describe their composition, role, and relationships.

FACILITIES AND RESOURCES

Describe the capabilities of the institution sponsoring the research, and document the availability of the facilities and other resources necessary to carry out the project. List the specific facilities available, including the following if they are appropriate to the project:

  office space and office equipment
  field locations
  computer resources
  backup administrative and research staff support
  library resources
  filing and storage facilities
  evidence of institutional commitment

Avoid using institutional "boiler-plate" descriptions. Instead, adapt them to the individual project.

BUDGET

The general guidelines for the preparation of the budget for a research proposal are the same as for other types of proposals, already presented in Chapter 5, and are not repeated here.

There are some aspects of budget preparation that are especially applicable to research budgets, particularly when they are sponsored by academic institutions and when they are submitted to federal funding agencies. Most universities and colleges have research offices that establish the rules for budget presentation, cost sharing, and charging overhead (indirect expenses), and that assist researchers in this part of the task. One can expect that the application forms for most government research programs will call for more detail than foundations require.

RESEARCH RESOURCES

The following are some of the specialized resources that can be used in developing research proposals.

PROPOSAL WRITING

The best single publication exclusively on research proposals, but limited to behavioral science research, is:

David R. Krathwohl, *How to Prepare a Research Proposal,* 2nd edition (Syracuse, N.Y.: Syracuse University Bookstore, 1977), 112 pages.

Other helpful material can be found in various issues of *Grants Magazine,* New York Plenum. A number of issues include sample research proposals.

For graduate students preparing dissertation proposals, a helpful reference might be:

Laurence F. Locke and Warren Wyrick Spirduso, *Proposals that Work: A Guide for Planning Research* (New York: Teachers College Press, 1976), 237 pages.

RESEARCH DESIGN AND METHODOLOGY

There are numerous good books on social research. Some examples are:

Claire Selitz, Lawrence S. Wrightsman, Stuart W. Cook, *Research Methods in Social Relations,* 3rd edition (New York: Holt, Rinehart and Winston, 1976), 624 pages.

Earl R. Babbie, *The Practice of Social Research* (Belmont, Calif.: Wadsworth Publishing Company, 1975), 511 pages.

7

Resources for Locating Funding Sources and Presenting Proposals

We shall now describe some of the resources available that can be utilized by proposal writers in preparing proposals and locating funding sources.

IDENTIFYING POTENTIAL FUNDING SOURCES— BASIC RESOURCES

There are a number of published reports, books, and periodicals that can be used to identify possible funding sources that would be responsive to a proposal. Many of these are very long and extensive. Some are quite helpful. Others provide only minimal information. The most helpful resources are so noted in the following descriptions. They will provide leads for followup. None of them will do the job by itself. Following up leads is time consuming, but it pays off. Because of the very large number of possible sources, one must try to be as selective as possible. A lot of material must be reviewed and then one has to concentrate on the more promising possibilities. The following are most widely used and helpful resources in the human service field:

The Grantsmanship Center News, published by the Grantsmanship Center, 1015 West Olympic Boulevard, Los Angeles, California 90015 ($20 subscription for six issues per year).

Excellent ongoing source of information on both governmental and foundation funding sources, grantsmanship, grant management, and proposal writing. The Grantsmanship Center also conducts training programs in many cities. Tuition is $375. The Center will send you information about these programs on request. The Center is a non-profit, tax-exempt, educational institution "committed to enhancing the quality of human service programs . . ."

The Foundation Center, 888 Seventh Avenue, New York, New York 10019.

The Foundation Center is an excellent resource for obtaining information about foundations. Its outstanding main library in its New York City headquarters has comprehensive current information on foundations, as do its Washington, D.C., Cleveland, and San Francisco reference collections. These centers and their collections are open to the public; so are their cooperating collections, located throughout the country.

A number of publications of the Foundation Center are described below. The listing of its national and cooperating collections is in Appendix B. Its four main reference collections are:

The Foundation Center   The Foundation Center
888 Seventh Avenue   1001 Connecticut Avenue, N.W.
New York, New York 10019   Washington, D.C. 20036

The Foundation Center   The Foundation Center
Kent H. Smith Library   312 Sutter Street
739 National City Bank Building   San Francisco, California 94108
629 Euclid
Cleveland, Ohio 44114

The Center also publishes a number of bibliographies in the grants field which are available free or at a modest charge. It maintains a national toll-free telephone service at 800-424-9836. It also provides a complete listing of directories that describe the foundations in each state. A summary of this information is in Appendix C.

Locating foundation possibilities requires a great deal of scanning and searching. The resources for identifying foundation possibilities are quite different from those used for locating government programs. Among the more widely used directories are *The Foundation Directory, The Foundation Grants Index,* and *The Foundation Center National Data Book*, all of which are publications of the Foundation Center.

The Foundation Directory, 7th edition, The Foundation Center, Columbia University Press, 136 South Broadway, Irvington, New York 10533; $40.

The basic reference guide to the foundation field. The Directory lists 3,200 foundations with assets of $1 million or more (or grants over $100,000). Also available are semiannual supplements to the Directory, listing other, smaller foundations, and giving information on changes among foundations listed in the Directory. Foundations are indexed by geographical coverage as well as by fields of interest. An example of the material found in the directory is shown in Figure 11.

Figure 11A.   From *The Foundation Directory*, 7th Edition, New York, 1979. Reprinted courtesy of The Foundation Center, New York, N.Y.

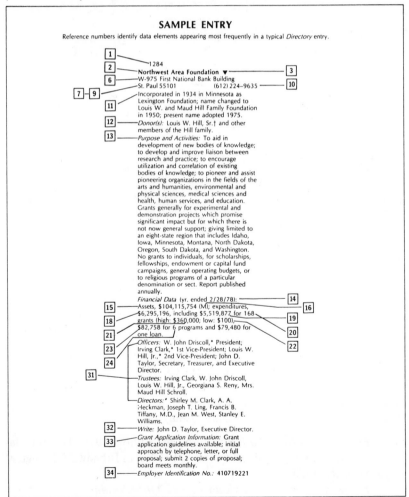

[1] Entry number. Locator number used in the indices.

[2] Foundation name. The full legal name of the foundation, often transposed to provide proper alphabetical order.

[3] ▼ Identifies foundations for which in-depth descriptions have been prepared for inclusion in *Foundation Center Source Book Profiles* (see Introduction, p. xi).

[4] Former name. Name under which the foundation has previously operated.

[5] Care of (name). Name of an institution or of an individual which should be included in the address to assure delivery of mail.

[6] Street address.

[7] City.

[8] State.

[9] Zip code.

[10] Telephone number. Supplied by the foundation.

[11] Establishment data. Legal form, usually a trust or corporation, and the year and the state in which organized.

[12] Donor name(s). Name(s) of the principal contributor(s) to the foundation, including individuals, families, and/or corporations. If a donor is deceased, the symbol † follows the name.

[13] Purpose and Activities. For the statement of purpose foundations frequently quote Section 501 (c) (3) of the Internal Revenue Code: "...organized and operated exclusively for religious, charitable, scientific, testing for public safety, literary, or educational purposes, or for the prevention of cruelty to children or animals...." When this or similar phrasing is used, it is condensed to read "Broad purposes," or, if "religion" is excluded, "General purposes." In the absence of a clearly defined statement of activities from the foundation, a description is composed on the basis of information appearing on the IRS returns. When the giving is largely confined to the area or state in which the foundation is located, the phrase "primarily local giving"

is applied. If the foundation does not make grants to individuals or, for example, for building or endowment purposes, the statement continues with "No grants to individuals or for building or endowment funds." More detailed restrictions are listed if supplied by the foundation. Finally, if the foundation publishes or issues a report, the paragraph concludes with "Report published [issued] annually" (or "biennially," "every five years," etc.).

[14] Fiscal year date. The year-end date of the foundation's accounting period.

[15] Asset amount. The total value of the foundation's investments. In a few instances, net worth is supplied when the total of mortgages and notes payable and other liabilities exceeds assets by more than ten percent.

[16] Asset type (Market or Ledger value). Generally the asset amount is reported at the market value at the year-end date of the foundation's accounting period.

[17] Gifts received. The amount of new capital received by the foundation in the year of record.

[18] Expenditures. The total disbursements of the foundation, including overhead expenses (salaries, investment, legal, and other professional fees, interest, taxes, rent, and other expenses), federal excise tax, and total grants, matching gifts, scholarships, loans, and/or programs paid.

[19] Grants amount. The total amount of grants paid within the year of record. It does not include commitments for payment in future years.

[20] Number of grants. The number of institutions (or individuals) to which grants were paid.

[21] High grant. The largest typical grant payment.

[22] Low grant. The minimum typical grant payment.

[23] Program amount. In addition to or instead of making grants, some foundations expend funds for internally administered programs.

[24] Number of programs. Some foundations may specify the number of different programs administered internally.

[25] Matching gifts amount. This generally relates to company-sponsored foundations which match employees' gifts, usually to educational institutions.

[26] Number of matching gifts.

[27] Scholarship amount. In addition to or instead of making grants, some foundations award scholarships to individuals.

[28] Number of scholarships.

[29] Loan amount. Usually educational loans to students.

[30] Number of loans.

[31] Names and titles of officers and trustees or directors. Some officers may also be trustees and/or directors. When this is the case, an asterisk (*) follows the name of the person.

[32] Write. The name of the person to whom inquiries for information or applications for grants, scholarships, or loans should be addressed.

[33] Grant Application Information. Rules for applying for a grant, month(s) in which the foundation prefers to receive applications, application deadlines, if any, number of copies required, and frequency and dates of board meetings.

[34] Employer Identification No. A number assigned by IRS which is useful in ordering filmed records or paper copies of Forms 990-PF and 990-AR from the Internal Revenue Service.

[35] Fields of interest. Index terms selected from the Purpose and Activities paragraph. See "Index of Fields of Interest."

[36] Limitations. Identifies foundations whose giving is primarily local within the city or state in which they are located. See "Index of Foundations by City and State."

[37] Foundation type. Identifies company-sponsored, operating, or community foundations.

Figure 11B. From *The Foundation Directory*, 7th Edition, New York, 1979. Reprinted courtesy of the Foundation Center, New York, N.Y.

Corporate Foundation Profiles, The Foundation Center, 888 Seventh Avenue, New York, New York 10019. $50.

Analyzes over 200 of the largest corporate-sponsored foundations and provides brief profiles on some 300 other corporate foundations. A good guide to this potential funding resource.

Foundation Grants to Individuals, 2nd edition, 1979, The Foundation Center, Columbia University Press, 136 South Broadway, Irvington, New York 10533; $15.

Listing of grants to individuals by 950 foundations.

The Foundation Center National Data Book: 4th edition, Volumes 1 and 2, The Foundation Center, Columbia University Press, 136 South Broadway, Irvington, New York 10533; $45 per set, 1116 pages.

Directory containing brief entries for more than 22,000 grant-making foundations, based on Internal Revenue Service records. Listing name, address, amount of assets and grants, IRS identification number, principal officer, availability of annual reports, and procedures for obtaining IRS records and using Foundation Center libraries. Cross indexed for locating states and cities.

Judith B. Margolin, *About Foundations: How to Find the Facts You Need to Get a Grant*, 1975, The Foundation Center, address as listed; 48 pages.

Excellent guide for grant seekers on how to efficiently use the resources of the Foundation Center library.

Carol M. Kurzig, *Foundation Fundamentals: A Guide for Grant-seekers*, 1980, The Foundation Center, 888 Seventh Avenue, New York, New York 10019; $4.95, 130 pages.

A complete manual on how to understand and research founda-tions and how to approach them. Also updates and expands About Foundations.

Two publications of the Center that are directed at the evaluation component of the proposal are:

Conducting Evaluations: Three Perspectives, 1980; $2.95, 50 pages.

Directory of Evaluation Consultants, 1980; $8.95, 375 pages.

The Foundation Center also annually publishes over 100 topical *Comsearch Printouts* extracted from the *Foundation Grants Index*, in-cluding human-service related topics such as education, health, welfare and population groups.

The Foundation Center also offers a variety of specialized services for locating funding sources. These include its "associates program" providing toll-free telephone reference service, taped bulletins on latest foundation news, a mail reference service, a computer-search service, copying services, and library-research services. The center also provides analytic profiles on 1,000 foundations as part of the *Foundation Source Book Profiles* (fee: $200).

Resources for locating governmental funding sources are not cen-tralized. A number of bills have been introduced in the U.S. Congress to improve the accessibility of information about federal funding programs available to local and state governments and nongovernmental organizations and agencies. The most recent version of these bills, the Federal Program Information Act, would require all federal agencies to report information on federal assistance programs to the Office of Management and Budget (OMB). This information is available to the public through a computerized search system, FAPRS, that is, the Federal Assistance Program Retrieval System. This system will go beyond the availability of information now included in the *Catalog of Federal Domestic Assistance*, which contains information submitted voluntarily.

The major resources for identifying federal programs are:

Federal Assistance Programs Retrieval System.
A computer-based information program of sources of federal funds. Originally developed by the U.S. Department of Agriculture, FAPRS is now the responsibility of the Office of Management and Budget. Access to FAPRS is available through regional offices of federal agencies, some libraries and universities, and some state and county government offices. OMB will provide the address of the nearest access point. Contact OMB, Budget Review Division, Federal Program Information Branch, Washington, D.C., 20503.

1980 Catalog of Federal Domestic Assistance, OMB, U.S. Government Printing Office, Washington, D.C. 20402; $20.
This is the major index of federal government domestic-assistance and grant programs. It is published by the Office of Management and Budget (OMB) and it includes over 1,000 assistance programs administered by 58 agencies. It also includes directions for use of the catalog, procedures to be followed by organizations seeking grants, and OMB and Treasury Department requirements that affect many of the federal programs listed. Directory information of the type listed in the catalog is outdated quickly and program descriptions are not uniformly informative. Eligibility for the various programs of nonprofit organizations, state and local governments, as well as individuals is referenced. It includes criteria for funding and a proposal outline. The catalog is available in most libraries and in federal and congressional offices. An example from the Catalog *is shown in Figure 12.*

Another source of information that can be used in tracking down federal programs is:

United States Government Manual, Government Printing Office, Washington, D.C. 20402; $6.50.
The government's guidebook of information about U.S. Government agencies, programs, and key officials.

13.628 CHILD ABUSE AND NEGLECT PREVENTION AND TREATMENT
(Child Abuse)

FEDERAL AGENCY: OFFICE OF HUMAN DEVELOPMENT SERVICES, DEPARTMENT OF HEALTH, EDUCATION, AND WELFARE

AUTHORIZATION: The Child Abuse Prevention and Treatment Act Title I, as amended, Public Law 93-247. (42 U.S.C. 5101 et seq.)

OBJECTIVES: To assist State, local, and voluntary agencies and organizations to strengthen their capacities to develop programs that will prevent, identify, and treat child abuse and neglect.

TYPES OF ASSISTANCE: Project Grants; Research Contracts.

USES AND USE RESTRICTIONS: Grants or contracts are for: (1) providing technical assistance to public and nonprofit private agencies and organizations; (2) demonstration programs and projects to develop and establish multi-disciplinary training programs; to establish and maintain centers to provide a broad range of activities including parent self-help in order to prevent, identify and treat child abuse and neglect. State grants are made to assist states in developing, strengthening and carrying out child abuse and neglect prevention and treatment programs; (3) research into the causes and prevention and treatment of child abuse and neglect. JOINT FUNDING: This program is considered suitable for joint funding with closely related Federal financial assistance programs in accordance with the provisions of OMB Circular No. A-111. For programs that are not identified as suitable for joint funding, the applicant may consult the headquarters or field office of the appropriate funding agency for further information on statutory or other restrictions involved.

ELIGIBILITY REQUIREMENTS:

Applicant Eligibility: Grants: State or local government or other nonprofit institutions of higher learning, State or local government or other private nonprofit agencies or organizations engaged in activities related to the prevention, identification, or treatment of child abuse and neglect. Contracts: Public and private organizations. State Grants: Those states qualifying under the provisions of Section 4(b)(2) of the Act.

Beneficiary Eligibility: Abused or neglected children and their families.

Credentials/Documentation: State Grant applications require certification of State's eligibility under Section 4(b)(2) of the Act; nonprofit organizations which have not previously received OHDS program support must submit proof of nonprofit status; applicable costs and administrative procedures will be determined in accordance with Part 74 of Title 45 of the Code of Federal Regulations.

APPLICATION AND AWARD PROCESS:

Preapplication Coordination: Technical assistance available at regional and national level to assist states in meeting qualifying conditions specified in the Act. Limited consultation available at headquarters office. Standard application forms provided by the Federal agency must be used. The standard applications forms as furnished by the Federal agency and required by OMB Circular No. A-102 must be used for this program. Applications are subject to State and areawide clearinghouses review pursuant to procedures in Part I, Attachment A of OMB Circular No. A-95 (revised).

Application Procedure: Demonstration and research applications, must use application forms provided by ACYF, these are to be submitted to Headquarters office. State grant applications to be submitted to the regional offices. This program is subject to the provisions of OMB Circular No. A-110.

Award Procedure: Research and demonstration grant applications reviewed by at least three non-Federal professionals with expertise in the field of child and family development, child welfare and child abuse and neglect. Final decision by Commissioner for Children, Youth and Families. State grant applications reviewed at Regional level with disapproval authority retained by Commissioner for Children, Youth and Families. Notification of awards must be made to the designated State Central Information Reception Agency in accordance with Treasury Circular 1082.

Deadlines: As specified in the announcement or application instructions.

Range of Approval/Disapproval Time: As specified in the announcement.

Appeals: Noné for research and demonstration applications. Not applicable to State Grants.

Renewals: Project renewals and extensions available through formal submission of progress reports and continuation applications. State grants require annual submission of application.

ASSISTANCE CONSIDERATIONS:

Formula and Matching Requirements: For research grants only recipients are required to provide at least 5 percent of the total direct costs on research grants.

Length and Time Phasing of Assistance: Research and Demonstration grants 1 to 4 years. Funding for each year after the first is subject to annual approval. State grants for single year.

POST ASSISTANCE REQUIREMENTS:

Reports: Financial and progress reports annually; final report and final expenditure report at completion of project.

Audits: Periodic audits should be made as part of the recipient systems of financial management and internal control to meet terms and conditions of grants and other agreements.

Records: All financial records are to be maintained 3 years after termination of the project or until audit is completed, whichever occurs first.

FINANCIAL INFORMATION:

Account Identification: 75-1636-0-1-500.

Obligations: FY 79 $18,891,000; FY 80 $22,928,000; and FY 81 est $22,928,000. NOTE: The funds in this program are also available for program contracts. The amounts which can be used for such contracts cannot be predetermined.

Range and Average of Financial Assistance: Average research and demonstration grant $100,000. Range from $30,000 to $300,000. State grants vary depending upon child population to be served.

PROGRAM ACCOMPLISHMENTS: Established as a part of the Children's Bureau, the National Center on Child Abuse and Neglect. In fiscal year 1978, the program funded 70 demonstrations that reached over 25,000 persons, trained over 18,000 professionals and para-professionals in positions related to child abuse and neglect services, and through grants to the more than 45 eligible states, served over 30,000 children and families.

REGULATIONS, GUIDELINES, AND LITERATURE: Regulations 45 CFR Part 1340, and 45 CFR Part 220, OHDS Grants Administrations Manuals available at no charge.

INFORMATION CONTACTS:

Regional or Local Office: Persons are encouraged to communicate with the Regional Program Directors, Children, Youth and Families, Office of Human Development Services, Department of Health, Education and Welfare, within each Regional Office. (See Appendix IV for a list of addresses of the regional offices.)

Headquarters Office: Director, National Center on Child Abuse and Neglect, Children's Bureau, P. O. Box 1182, Washington, DC 20013. Telephone: (202) 755-0591.

RELATED PROGRAMS: 13.600, Administration for Children, Youth and Families—Head Start; 13.608, Administration for Children, Youth and Families—Child Welfare Research and Demonstration Grants; 13.645, Child Welfare Services—State Grants; 13.648, Training Grants in the Field of Child Welfare.

EXAMPLES OF FUNDED PROJECTS: Child Abuse and Neglect Resource Demonstration; Abuse and Neglect Among Low Income Families; Urban Indian Child Resource Center; Child Abuse and Neglect Service Project.

CRITERIA FOR SELECTING PROPOSALS: Degree to which the proposal promises to meet the specific objectives defined, in the annual program announcement; reasonableness of cost; qualifications of staff; and for State grants, eligibility of the State as determined by HEW.

Figure 12. An example from the *Catalog of Federal Domestic Assistance.*

Two more resources to be used in the search for available government funds are the *Commerce Business Daily* and *The Federal Register.*

Commerce Business Daily, U.S. Department of Commerce, Superintendent of Documents, Government Printing Office, Washington, D.C. 20402; $105.
Daily listing of government procurements, potential contracts, awards, and so on.

Federal Register, published five days per week. Superintendent of Documents, U.S. Government Printing Office, Washington, D.C. 20402.
Reports guidelines and regulations for government programs.

SUPPLEMENTAL RESOURCES FOR IDENTIFYING FUNDING SOURCES

In addition to the resources described above there are numerous other directories and services that can be utilized to locate possible funding sources. These include the following:

An Analysis of Federal R & D Funding by Function, 1976, U.S. Government Printing Office, Washington, D.C. 20402; $2.45, 76 pages (single copies free from the National Science Foundation).
Classifies by function the trends in federal support for research and development activities including health, education, income security, social services, crime prevention and control, community development, housing and public services, environment, transportation, and natural resources.

Annual Register of Grant Support, 1980–81, Marquis Academic Media, 200 East Ohio Street, Chicago, Illinois 60611; $57.50, 751 pages.
Lists information on grants to individuals and organizations from governmental agencies, foundations, corporations, and other groups.

Lilly Cohen and Marie Oppedisano-Reich, *A National Guide to Government and Foundation Funding Sources in the Field of Aging*, 1977, Adelphi University Press, Garden City, New York 11530; 174 pages.
A basic reference guide to both public and private funding sources for programs related to older people.

Corporate Foundation Directory, 1979–80, Taft Corporation, Washington, D.C.; 446 pages.

A directory of selected corporate foundations and sponsoring companies with basic descriptive information.

Corporate Fund Raising Directory, 1980–81, 1st edition, Public Service Materials Center, 415 Lexington Avenue, New York, New York 10017; $19.75.

A listing that describes some 350 corporations and corporate foundations.

The Complete Grants Sourcebook for Higher Education, American Council on Education, One Dupont Circle, Washington, D.C. 20036; $79.

Information on over 500 funding sources for higher education programs and a description of methods for seeking funds.

The CFAE Casebook: Aid-To-Education Programs of Leading Business Concerns and Guidelines for Corporate Support of Higher Education, 1974, Council for Financial Aid to Education, Inc. 680 Fifth Avenue, New York, New York 10019; $9.00, 211 pages.

An examination of corporate support for education aimed at helping companies structure aid-to-education programs. Includes a directory of corporate programs and grants to education.

Joseph Dermer, *Where America's Large Foundations Make Their Grants*, 1980–81 edition, Public Service Materials Center, 415 Lexington Avenue, New York, New York 10017; $34.50.

Lists foundation grants and offers suggestions on grantsmanship and proposal writing.

Federal Grants and Contracts Weekly, Capitol Publications, Inc., 2430 Pennsylvania Avenue, N.W., Washington, D.C. 20037.

Weekly announcement of programs available to support education programs and human services.

Health Grants and Contracts Weekly, Capitol Publications, Inc., same as above.

Weekly announcement of programs available to support health programs.

Human Resources Network, *The Handbook of Corporate Social Responsibility: Profiles of Involvement*, 1975, Chilton Book Company, Chilton Way, Radnor, Pennsylvania 19089; 62 pages.

A description of 743 projects supported by 231 corporations.

Human Resources Network, *User's Guide to Funding Resources*, 1975, Chilton Book Company, Chilton Way, Radnor, Pennsylvania 19089; 231 pages.

Describes funding programs of public and private agencies, foundations, and corporations.

James Klevens, "Researching Foundations: An Inside View of What They Are and How They Operate," *Chronica*, Volume 11, No. 2, (March–April 1977), Research Foundation of the State University of New York, Albany, New York 12201.

Guidelines for identifying foundation resources. Stresses the importance of initially approaching foundations with a brief (two- or three-page) letter explaining the proposal.

Local Government Funding Report, Government Information Services, 752 National Press Building, Washington, D.C. 20004 (biweekly).

A good guide to developments in governmental funding programs.

Looking for a Grant: A Kit for Groups Seeking Financial Assistance, 1975, U.S. Department of Labor, Employment Standards Administration, Women's Bureau, Washington, D.C. 20210; 40 pages.

Resources for women's groups seeking funds.

Network of Change Oriented Foundations, Playboy Foundation, 919 North Michigan Avenue, Chicago, Illinois 60611; free.

A listing of foundations with a special interest in social change projects.

1978 Foundation 500, Foundation Research Service, 39 East 51st Street, New York, New York 10012.

Index of the 500 top foundations.

The 1980–81 Survey of Grant-Making Foundations, Public Service Materials Center, 415 Lexington Avenue, New York, New York 10017.

A listing of basic descriptive data on over 1,000 larger foundations.

1980 Directory of Federal Health/Medicine Grants and Contracts Programs, Science and Health Publications, Bethesda, Maryland.

A listing of health and related programs from the Catalog of Federal Domestic Assistance.

Oryx Press, 3930 East Camelback Road, Phoenix, Arizona 85018.

Publishes a series of directories and information systems (mostly applicable to colleges and universities) regarding federal, state, and local governmental agencies, foundations, and other sources for research, training, programs, and "innovative efforts."

These include the following:

Directory of Research Grants, 1980 edition; $39.50.

Lists some 2,000 grant programs from foundations, public agencies, and corporations for research and service programs.

Grant Information System; $425.

Four loose-leaf quarterly reports and a monthly newsletter of available programs with deadline dates, entitled "Faculty Alert Bulletins."

Public Health Service Profiles of Financial Assistance Programs, U.S. Department of Health and Human Services, U.S. Government Printing Office, Washington, D.C. 20402; 105 pages.
Describes specific programs of the Public Health Service that provide grants and contracts for research and service projects in the health field based on the Catalog of Federal Domestic Assistance *material.*

U.S. Foundations and Minority-Group Interests, 1975, U.S. Human Resources Corporation, San Francisco, California; 299 pages.
A study of foundation support for minority programs.

The Science Information Exchange, Smithsonian Institution, Washington, D.C. 20560.
Abstracts of information on research and action programs.

Gail Ann Schlachter, *Directory of Financial Aids for Women,* 1978, Reference Service Press, 9023 Alcott Street, Los Angeles, California 90035; $15.95, 200 pages.
A listing of a wide range of funding sources that are intended to support women's activities.

Taft Information System Foundation Reporter, Taft Corporation, Inc., 1000 Vermont Avenue, N.W., Washington, D.C. 20005.
Taft, a commercial firm, publishes a number of publications and offers a number of services aimed at providing basic information on foundation funding sources. These include a monthly News Monitor, and Trustees of Wealth: A Biographical Directory of Private Foundation and Corporate Foundation Officers.

GRANTSMANSHIP RESOURCES

Listed here are a number of selected publications that are aimed at improving an understanding of the grants process and at developing skills in seeking funds and writing proposals.

The Bread Game, revised edition, 1974, Glide Publications, 330 Ellis Street, San Francisco, California 94102; 96 pages.
A popularly written guide to the grantsmanship process with a special emphasis on social-change oriented programs, third-world community, and responsible grant-management methods.

Jean Brodsky, editor, *The Proposal Writer's Swipe File II,* 1976, Taft Products, Washington, D.C.; $9.95.
Contains 14 sample proposals.

John D. Callen, James C. Marillo, and Joseph T. Nocerino, *The Process of Grantsmanship and Proposal Development,* 1976, Century Planning Associates, Inc., Vienna, Virginia 22180; 98 pages.
A workbook and manual intended to help individuals understand the process of grantsmanship and proposal development and participate in it.

Daniel Lynn Conrad, et al., *The Grants Planner,* 1979, Public Management Institute, 333 Haynes Street, San Francisco, California 94102; 256 pages.
A loose-leaf notebook on techniques to grantsmanship based on a variety of forms and worksheets.

Lois DeBakey, "The Persuasive Proposal," *Foundation News,* Volume 18, No. 4 (July–August, 1977), Council on Foundations, Inc., 888 Seventh Avenue, New York, New York 10019.
A review of principles for preparing persuasive proposals related to research and scientific investigation; it focuses on the precision, conciseness, and other methods to facilitate sound proposal writing.

Joseph Dermer, *How to Write Successful Foundation Presentations,* 1972, Public Service Materials Center, 415 Lexington Avenue, New York, New York 10017; $9.95, 80 pages.
Guidelines to preparing proposals for foundations.

Joseph Dermer, *The New How To Raise Funds From Foundations,* Public Service Materials Center, same as above; $9.95.
How to approach foundations and prepare proposals.

Philip Des Marais, *How to Get Government Grants,* 1975, Public Service Materials Center, 415 Lexington Avenue, New York, New York 10017.
Explains types of government grants such as entitlement, formula, and project grants, and ways to pursue these possibilities.

Burton J. Eckstein, editor, *Handicapped Funding Directory, 1980–81,* Research Grant Guides, P.O. Box 357, Oceanside, New York 11572; $16.50, 172 pages.
A series of good articles on various aspects of the grant process. Lists foundations and government agencies that provide grant funds to institutions and agencies for programs and services for the handicapped.

The Foundation News, Council on Foundations, Inc., 1828 L Street, N.W., Washington, D.C. 20036.

A periodical that includes articles on foundation funding, news about what is going on among foundations, and a monthly listing of specific foundation grants that have been made which become included in the Foundation Center's Grants Index.

Grants Magazine: The Journal of Sponsored Research and Other Programs, Plenum Press, New York, New York.
An interesting periodical with a range of articles and a helpful grants clinic with sample proposals. Quarterly.

Giving in America: Toward a Stronger Voluntary Sector, 1975, Commission on Private Philanthropy and Public Needs, 1776 K Street, N.W., Washington, D.C. 20036; $1.50, 240 pages.
A frequently quoted useful study of philanthropy. Popularly known as the "Filer Report."

Mary Hall, *Developing Skills in Proposal Writing,* 2nd edition, 1979, Continuing Education Publications, Portland, Oregon; $12.50, 194 pages.
One of the better popular books on proposal writing that includes a comprehensive explanation of what to include in each section of the proposal.

David Hawkridge, Reggie L. Campeau, and Penelope K. Trickett, *Preparing Evaluation Reports: A Guide for Authors,* 1970, American Institutes for Research, 4614 Fifth Avenue, Pittsburgh, Pennsylvania 15200; $1.25, 68 pages.
Prepared under contract with the Department of Health, Education, and Welfare, this publication outlines specific ways to report on the results of evaluation on education programs. It contains good examples, which can also serve as useful guides to proposal preparation.

Jean L. Hennessey, "The Unpersuasive Proposal," *Foundation News,* Volume 18, No. 4 (July–August, 1977), Council on Foundations, Inc., 888 Seventh Avenue, New York, New York 10019.
Outlines how foundations can respond to proposals that do not fit their purposes by going beyond rejection of the proposal and considering other alternative responses.

Howard Hillman and Karin Abarbanel, *The Art of Winning Foundation Grants,* 1975, Vanguard Press, Inc., 424 Madison Avenue, New York, New York 10017; $6.95, 188 pages.
Guidelines for approaching foundations and an examination of proposal-writing methods.

Howard Hillman, *The Art of Winning Corporate Grants,* 1980, Vanguard Press, Inc., as above.
Guidelines for the growing field of corporate giving, including a

description of how corporate giving works, how to approach corporations, and preparing proposals for corporations.

David R. Krathwohl, *How to Prepare a Research Proposal*, 2nd edition, 1977, Syracuse University Bookstore, 303 University Place, Syracuse, New York 13210; $3.95, 112 pages.
One of the better guides to preparation of research proposals in the behavioral-science area.

Norman J. Kiritz, *Program Planning and Proposal Writing*, The Grantsmanship Center, 1015 West Olympic Boulevard, Los Angeles, California 90015; $2.45, 48 pages.
A good guide to basic ingredients of a program proposal. The Grantsmanship News, noted above, is also a fine resource for information on all aspects of the grant-seeking and grant-management process. A smaller eight-page version is also available for $.95.

The Philanthropy Monthly, Non-Profit Report, Inc., P.O. Box 989, New Milford, Connecticut 06776.
A periodical of news of the field of philanthropy and specific articles on management and operations of nonprofit agencies.

Public Health Service Grants Policy Statement, 1976, Department of Health and Human Services, U.S. Government Printing Office, Washington, D.C. 20402; 92 pages.
Explains the manner in which the Public Health Service and its component agencies (the Alcohol, Drug Abuse, and Mental Health Administration, the Center for Disease Control, the Food and Drug Administration, the Health Resources Administration, the Health Services Administration, and the National Institutes of Health) administer a diverse array of grant programs requiring adherence to both program objectives and "effective business management systems."

Craig W. Smith and Eric W. Skjei, *Getting Grants*, 1980, Harper and Row, New York, New York; 286 pages.
A popularized general survey of the grants field that emphasizes approaches to identify and approach funders. A good deal of editorial comment on the various institutions related to the grants field.

Special Report on Hispanics and Grantmakers, 1981, Council on Foundations; $5.95, 120 pages.
A report on a series of meetings devoted to issues involved in grant support for Hispanic programs. Can be ordered from Fulfillment Services, 7212 Lockport Place, Lorton, Virginia 22079.

Virginia P. White, *Grants: How to Find Out about Them and What to Do Next*, 1975, Plenum Publishing Corporation, 227 West 17th Street, New York, New York 10011; $19.50, 354 pages.

A thorough examination of the grantsmanship process as it applies to the search for government grants, foundation grants, and business and industry grants. Considered by many as one of the better comprehensive guides to the field.

Virginia P. White, *Grants for the Arts*, 1980, Plenum Publishing Corporation, as above; $19.50, 378 pages.

How to locate grant sources for the arts and a description of the principles and methods that apply to the pre-application, application, and post-application phases of grant seeking, using the same approach as in Grants.

RESOURCES FOR USE IN PREPARING NEEDS AND PROGRAM SECTIONS

The following are among the materials helpful in preparing those parts of the proposal that are directed at defining the problem and need for the proposed program, and in developing program philosophy, objectives, strategy, and activities:

Statistical Abstract of the United States, Bureau of the Census, U.S. Department of Commerce, U.S. Government Printing Office, Washington, D.C. 20402.
Summary statistics on population, health and social services, prevalence of health and social conditions, and government expenditures.

Social Indicators, prepared by the Office of Management and Budget, U.S. Government Printing Office, Washington, D.C. 20402.
Basic statistics indicative of social health and economic conditions.

U.S. Decennial Census, Bureau of the Census, U.S. Department of Commerce, U.S. Government Printing Office, Washington, D.C. 20402.

Current Population Surveys, Bureau of the Census, U.S. Department of Commerce, same address.

Labor force data are available from the U.S. Department of Labor, Bureau of Labor Statistics, 441 G Street, N.W., Washington, D.C. 20212.

The Statistical Reporter, published by the Office of Management and Budget, U.S. Government Printing Office, Washington, D.C. 20402.

Report of the President's Council of Economic Advisors, U.S. Government Printing Office, Washington, D.C. 20402.
Reports on economic indicators and conditions.

Employment and Training Report of the President, U.S. Government Printing Office, Washington, D.C. 20402.

Basic statistics on manpower, employment, unemployment, and training programs.

Reports of various national commissions, legislative committees, task forces, and boards of inquiry can be found by checking local libraries for such reports in the field covered by the proposal. In addition, there are hundreds of pamphlets published by federal agencies on almost every type of program. One should check local libraries and write to the Department of Health and Human Services and the Government Printing Office for lists of available publications in one's field. Professional journals provide another source, which can be located with the help of a local reference librarian. The Grantsmanship Center has a bibliography of these materials; it can be obtained on request.

The annual reports of state and local agencies such as welfare, health, mental health, manpower, and youth-service agencies can be requested from those agencies. These reports often include considerable data on needs, service statistics, expenditures, and trends.

The Social Security Bulletin, published periodically by the Social Security Administration of the Department of Health and Human Services, is a good source of national statistics in health and welfare.

State and local planning commissions and agencies, chambers of commerce, legislative reference bureaus, and health and welfare councils also publish reports that will provide local demographic and substantive material regarding needs and services. Local banks and utilities conduct considerable demographic research and their reports may be available.

The source for quoted materials must always be indicated by using appropriate footnotes at the bottom of the page, and if material from private sources such as banks is quoted, permission for its use should be obtained.

8

Understanding and Approaching Funding Sources

In this chapter we discuss some of the principles and methods for approaching and cultivating potential funding sources. We also include an explanation of the difference between foundation and government funding programs. The chapter concludes with a description of when and how to prepare mini-proposals as a grant seeking device.

One must not hesitate to call and make appointments with program officers or other staff people at the various foundations identified. They can give important advice regarding their guidelines and policies, suggest program emphasis, and recommend other possible foundations. Much of this can be accomplished on the telephone, since only the large foundations have the staff resources to engage in a lot of personal interviews.

In addition, there is a federal agency for just about everything. These agencies have staff people located in their regional offices. The Department of Health and Human Services (including the National Institutes of Health) and the Department of Labor are the main sources of federal funds for most human service programs. A unit, office, or bureau of the department must be found whose scope of interest might cover the proposed activity. A regional staff person in this unit should be called. If they do not have an appropriate program, suggestions of other programs may be requested, in addition to explanatory publications regarding the programs of the various offices. It is advisable to call the regional director's office in order to find out which unit should be contacted first.

Federal employees and foundation staff are there to respond to public needs and demands. Most people fail to use these valuable resources.

Local universities and colleges often maintain "development" offices or research foundations that have a good deal of resource material that may be made available. There are also many professional fund-raising firms in large cities that, for a fee, engage in various fund-raising services. These are listed in the Yellow Pages of the telephone book.

It is important for agencies and organizations seeking and receiving government grants to be aware of government regulations and procedures that pertain to this type of support. A basic resource here is the Federal Office of Management and Budget's Circular A-95, revised, which explains rules under which agencies seeking federal money must engage in certain evaluation, review, and coordination procedures. The Office of Management and Budget, Executive Office Building, 17th Street and Pennsylvania Avenue, Washington, D.C. 20503, publishes a pamphlet, "Federal Circular A-95, What It Is and How It Works," and, "Federal Management Circular 74-7," explaining the administrative standards for financial management and reporting in connection with federal grants.

Senators and members of Congress may be involved in the process of identifying possible funding sources and obtaining resource material published by the federal government. At the state and local level local representatives may be involved in the same way.

As potential funding sources are identified and proposals developed, there is always the problem of deciding to whom the proposal must be sent. It is perfectly ethical to submit the same proposal to more than one funding source or to attempt to get joint or partial support from a number of different sources. One can be frank about this in dealing with funders.

There is also the problem of deciding on how much support might be requested. The range of possible support from any funding source can be ascertained in a number of ways:

1. Some funders have specific guidelines and limits on the amount of support they provide any project. They will tell this if asked.
2. By looking at the kinds of projects already supported and the amounts granted, one can make an estimate of the range of money that might be available for the proposed project. The various grant indexes, foundation reports, and government reports mentioned in this chapter provide some of this information. Again, the appropriate staff person in the government agency and foundation should be asked for this information. Under federal law one is entitled to the information.

There is no substitute for personal contact and visibility with funders so that they know whom they are dealing with; thus the proposal becomes more than a written document. However, these contacts must be kept brief and to the point.

These contacts can be made prior to submission of the proposal as well as after it is submitted. People experienced in grantsmanship often suggest that if one is not sure that the funder wants to receive the entire proposal, a summary statement should be sent first. If the response is favorable, the entire proposal can be submitted. Many foundations prefer this procedure so that they might ascertain whether the proposal is in their area of interest without having to review the entire proposal.

Often applicants will be asked to make a verbal presentation to supplement or explain the proposal. These must be prepared carefully. Applicants should not only be thoroughly familiar with their own material, but must also do some research regarding the funder in order to be able to demonstrate an understanding of the funder's interests and areas of support.

It is advisable to get on the mailing lists of various federal agencies that operate in the fields of interest to one's agency. One can get on the lists of many agencies by simply sending in a written request to this effect. An example of the kind of information needed by the funding agency, as called for in federal forms for this purpose, include:

1. applicant's name and address;
2. type of organization and area of interest;
3. names of officers;
4. kinds of programs on which applicants wish to bid;
5. size of organization.

Many government agencies send out materials to assist applicants in taking advantage of special programs. But one can receive this material only by being on the agency's mailing list.

SIMILARITIES AND DIFFERENCES BETWEEN FOUNDATIONS AND GOVERNMENT FUNDING SOURCES

When preparing a proposal to government funding sources, it must be kept in mind that there are five important factors that differentiate them from private foundations. First, proposals submitted to federal, state, county, city, town, or other local government agencies are requesting governmental or public (that is, tax) funds to support a particular program. Governmental monies are expended under specific legislative appropriations and authorizations that are expressed in laws, acts, bills, or resolutions of the legislative body (for instance, Congress, state assembly, county surpervisors, city council, and so on). These funds are only allocated through grants or contracts that are clearly within the legislative provisions that authorize their expenditure.

Second, in addition to the legislative authority to expend such funds, governmental funding agencies are guided by specific written rules and regulations and written guidelines that govern the administration of each program. These are usually drawn up by the government department, agency, or unit responsible for administering the program. They have been subjected to public hearings and then revised and adopted by the department. They are public documents, which are available upon request. The *Federal Register* can be checked for these materials.

Third, governmental agencies, particularly federal agencies, also prepare and print pamphlets and reports that explain the philosophy and approach of various specific government programs. These are also available upon request.

Fourth, another aspect of governmental funding is what is referred to as "legislative intent." This refers to the intentions of the legislative body that established a particular program when it passed a bill. The intent is reflected in statements made by legislative committees when they report out bills for approval; it can be found in committee reports. As public administrators move to implement these programs, they are guided, in part, by their understanding of this intent.

Fifth, most public agencies require that budgets and often the entire proposal be submitted on forms that they have devised for this purpose. Taken together, the laws, rules, regulations, guidelines, forms, programmatic reports, and programmatic philosophies establish the limits, priorities, and ground rules for making decisions about the allocation of public funds by governmental bodies. By studying them carefully one can assure that the proposal is responsive to and within the limits of what the public agency can legally support.

Foundations, on the other hand, are influenced in their funding decisions by a set of factors, some of which are similar and some of which are different from those that influence governmental funders. First, each foundation is incorporated as a nonprofit organization and, as such, has a set of general purposes and policies that establish the general nature and limitations on the kind of projects it may support. These purposes and policies sometimes represent the conditions set forth by the original donor(s) who established the foundation. In other cases they are established by the officers or board of directors of the foundation. Limits may be set by foundations on:

a. the type of program to be supported;
b. the geographical area within which the foundation may support programs;
c. the minimum or maximum amount that can be granted to any applicant;
d. the type of organization that can receive grants.

Since passage of the 1969 Federal Tax Reform Act and state legislation, foundations have become more cautious in their procedures and generally prefer to make grants only to incorporated nonprofit organizations. The Internal Revenue Service issues "letters of exemption" to groups, organizations, and agencies that conduct nonprofit operations. These letters, which are obtained through formal application to the Internal Revenue Service, serve to assure the foundation that the applying organization can legitimately receive foundation grants without imposing liability on the foundation. If the organization does not have an exemption letter, it is sometimes possible to have the proposed project sponsored by a larger established agency whose charitable religious or educational nonprofit status is already established and whose purposes are similar to those set forth in the proposal.

Final decisions or ratification with respect to grants are generally made by the foundation board or committees, based on review of the proposal by the foundation's paid staff members. In large foundations there may be a number of levels of staff review.[7] (In the case of government agencies, there are almost always at least two levels of staff review and the final decision is made by top bureau, unit, or departmental officials. In addition, many government agencies utilize review panels of expert consultants as part of their review and decision-making process.)

Foundations range from those that have a wide range of general purposes to those that have very specialized interests. In general, the larger the foundation, the wider its range of interests. By reviewing the *Foundation Directory*, requesting copies of the foundation's annual report of its grant support, and talking to others who are experienced in proposal writing and seeking foundation support, one can ascertain which foundations may be interested in the subject of the proposal. Selectivity is advised. There are over 25,000 foundations, many quite small, and it is certainly not feasible to review all of them.

[7]See Robert Mayer, "What Will a Foundation Look for When You Submit a Grant Proposal?" (New York: The Foundation Center, 1972. Available free.)

Support may be sought from more than one foundation at the same time, or, from both governmental and foundation sources at the same time. It is not unusual for promising projects in the human service field to obtain support from both these sources.

Corporations and corporate foundations also have special interests. Large corporate foundations operate much like other foundations. Corporate foundations are particularly interested in supporting projects that will reflect well on the reputation of the corporation. They also have a special interest in projects that will improve the quality of life in the communities in which they are located. It is important to keep in mind that both the government and foundations have funds that they *must* spend. Although funders may appear to be hard-nosed and resistant, and although there is considerable competition for the same dollars, there is still pressure on the funders to locate and support promising and credible programs.

Many foundations, whether they be large and of national scope or smaller ones that focus on supporting programs in their local community or state, prefer to support new programs and shy away from ongoing support for already established programs. This means that the proposal should clearly delineate the aspects of the proposed program or research that are innovative, new, and of a pilot or demonstration nature. It also means that the proposal should indicate concrete plans for continuation of the project after a period of foundation support. Governmental agencies are prone to avoid supporting ongoing programs as well, but not to the extent that this characterizes foundations; and, of course, many government programs are for ongoing support of specific activities as authorized by law. Government funders, more than foundations, are also constrained by the provisions of the formal guidelines and regulations that govern each program. A proposal to a governmental source should be responsive to these guidelines. Some foundations have also established certain priorities and program emphases that define more specifically than their statements of purpose the kinds of projects that they are interested in supporting. However, they often have more flexibility than most government agencies in their pattern of support. This does not necessarily mean that foundations are always the principal supporters of innovation, demonstration and experimentation. Actually, sometimes governmental agencies play this role, and at other times foundations do.

In addition to foundations and government agencies, there are other possible sources of support that should not be overlooked, such as labor unions, certain church groups, and community organizations and associations. These do not present major possibilities, since they offer rather limited resources. On a local basis, however, they may open possibilities for a proposed project.

There are a number of different types of interests that may appeal to governmental funding agencies or foundations, including:

1. *Problem solutions*—support of programs aimed at alleviating, reducing, or preventing particular social problems such as delinquency, family breakdown, mental illness, dependency, nutritional deficiencies, waste of resources, group conflict, and so on.
2. *Methodological demonstrations*—support of programs that will demonstrate, test, or assess particular strategies, methods, and techniques for solving problems, serving people, evaluating and managing programs, and so on.
3. *Institution building*—support to improve, extend, or strengthen existing agencies and organizations such as schools, orchestras, libraries, hospitals, and so on.
4. *Individual achievement*—support to individuals to carry out individual work that shows intellectual, cultural, scholarly, or artistic promise; or, to enable individuals to pursue further training in professional fields.
5. *Social-value contributions*—support for projects or work that has or may have intrinsic social value and benefit to society in general, such as basic research and education.

The fact that all these types of projects may be of interest to both governmental agencies and foundations serves to illustrate that any specific project may be suitable for support from either one of these sources. Both may be tried if the government program and foundation within whose scope of interest the program may fall can be located. Foundations and government agencies are so numerous and diverse that it is impossible to make more specific categorical statements that apply to all of them. Only research and experience can provide the specific information required to successfully pursue the funding sources most likely to respond to a proposal.

MINI-PROPOSALS

Some funding agencies prefer to review a brief proposal before a more complete, detailed proposal is submitted. A brief proposal is also often sufficient when one is requesting relatively small amounts of money—less than $5,000 or $10,000. Proposals of this kind may be referred to in a variety of ways by funders; the terms include "concept paper," "prospectus," "summary," "abstract," "synopsis," "letter of interest," "preliminary outline," "letter of inquiry," "project brief," and the like. The content of the mini-proposal may be presented entirely in the form of either a letter or a separate document submitted with a short covering letter. When in doubt, it is suggested to prepare it in the form of a brief, separate document as described below.

Mini-proposals serve a number of functions. They provide a device to facilitate the initial screening of requests by funders. This enables the funder to judge the extent to which the proposed project is eligible for funds and whether or not it is consistent with the funder's interests, goals, and priorities. It also may provide an opportunity for the funder to suggest modifications prior to submission of a complete proposal. The mini-proposal also provides a way to inquire about the possible interest of a number of different funders at the same time with a mimimum of paper work and preparation.

Some proposal writers recommend that the mini-proposal or letter should be submitted to funders whenever possible. However, unless the funding agency requires this as part of its funding process, as do some government agencies and foundations, there are some disadvantages to routinely employing the mini-proposal approach. Funders may be more inclined to disregard the receipt of a mini-proposal than of a complete proposal. Because of its brevity, it also has the disadvantage of possibly obscuring the impact or importance of a proposed project. Thus, one must weigh the pros and cons of this approach with considerable care. If in doubt, submit a more complete proposal with a good summary section as suggested in Chapter 5.

In cases where a mini-proposal is clearly desirable or required, the following guidelines may be followed in its preparation.

Length and Format

Make the mini-proposal a separate document from the letter of transmittal. It may range in length from one page to about five pages. In addition to a brief letter of transmittal:

> use some headings if the mini-proposal is more than two pages long,
> include a formal title for the project,
> use a cover page if the mini-proposal is three or more pages,
> do not use a table of contents,
> keep any attachments to a minimum,
> include a budget on a separate page.

What to Stress

A mini-proposal should have a minimum of eight key brief paragraphs, including:

- a paragraph on why the proposal should be of interest to the funder, i.e., its responsiveness or consistency with a specific aspect of the funder's stated goals, interest, or prior funding history
- a paragraph on what the proposal is about, where the proposed activities will take place, and for how long
- a paragraph describing the capability of the proposer
- a paragraph that states the major problem and need for the proposed project, and some key facts documenting the need or extent of the problem
- a paragraph that describes the overall purpose of the project and lists the major objectives
- a paragraph that provides the highlights of the major activities that will be undertaken
- a paragraph that describes the staff or personnel that would be involved
- a paragraph that explains the budget request

Attach to this mini-proposal a one-page, line-by-line budget request, unless the request is so small that it is self-explanatory, e.g., a request for $3,000 for the cost of printing a community service directory.

Appendix A: Sample Program Proposal and Critique

This appendix includes a sample program proposal accompanied by a critique pointing out its strengths and weaknesses. For illustrative purposes, a proposal to establish a multiservice center as a decentralized branch of a larger city-wide agency has been chosen. This clarifies most of the essential points and is typical of the various issues that must be addressed in many program proposals.* The sample proposal omits a budget and timetable since these are illustrated in Chapter 5.

*The sample proposal is based in part on material prepared by Polly Purvis. I am indebted to her for allowing me to adapt some of her work.

Proposal	Critique

TITLE PAGE

A Proposal to Establish
Community-Based Multiservice
Center

June 1981

Submitted by:
The Plainview
Service Organization
10 Plainview Avenue
Plainview, New York 11000
Telephone (516)516-5166

The format for this title page is good. It is descriptive, providing all the essential information. It does not show the funding source to whom it is submitted (optional). This could be done by placing an additional phrase after "submitted by, and so on," which would read:

Submitted to:
The ABC Foundation
10 Avenue L
New York, New York 10080

The title of the proposal, however, is misleading, since the larger part of the proposal that follows is addressed to establishing services that are alternatives to existing programs. Thus, the title would be more descriptive if the word "Alternative" were added before the words "Multiservice."

INTRODUCTION: PURPOSE AND OBJECTIVES

This is a proposal from the Plainview Service Organization (PSO) to establish a community-based multiservice center offering a variety of alternative mental health services to individuals, families, and the community in the town of Plainview, located in Plainview County, N.Y.

The PSO is a voluntary nonprofit agency which has served Plainview County, whose current population is 1 million, since 1945. Its total operating budget of $1 million comes from the United Fund and federal and state grants. Originally established as a family counseling and home nursing

A good opening sentence, which covers the name of the applicant, the general contents of the program, and its location.

The proposal attempts to establish PSO's credentials, without going into detail, in the body of the proposal. The detail is presented in a separate capability statement. The reader's attention is directed to the statement by footnote 7. Some proposal writers prefer a longer statement about the

agency, the PSO, for the last ten years, has changed its focus to concentrate on developing and demonstrating a variety of services aimed at meeting newly identified specialized needs of minorities, aged, and children.* This proposal is in keeping with this focus in that it addresses the emerging needs for preventive and advocacy programs in the field of mental health and particularly for released mental patients.

Through this proposed program a number of urgent needs in Plainview are addressed including, 1. the failure of existing agencies, particularly the Welfare Department and mental health clinics, to provide sorely needed prevention-oriented services, 2. the lack of direction of both state and county agencies in the area of mental health in Plainview, 3. the inability of these agencies to serve an advocacy role for minorities and the poor, 4. the frequently inaccessible and fragmenting nature of these programs, and 5. the absence of recognizable communities within Plainview to actually serve the social needs of residents.

These problems are further aggravated because of a lack of clarity over the definition of mental health and the causes of mental illness. The social implication of mental illness is the fact that individuals who are affected emotionally and psychologically by economic and social situations have been undermined or sponsoring organization at this point in the proposal.

The focus of the proposal on mental health is established early in the introduction. At this point the emphasis on prevention and on released mental patients is established, still very early in the proposal. It is done in a way to entice the reader to go further.

It is appropriate in the Introduction to briefly describe the nature of the problem that is being addressed, as is done here. However, in this proposal the problem is defined largely in terms of the limitations of existing agencies and theory or ideologies (that is, the definition of mental illness and its causes). The proposal would be strengthened with more specificity in the Introduction, such as the gross number of persons served by mental-health agencies, the number released from hospitals, the number requiring prevention, a specific example of "lack of direction" and other needs. Although all this will be dealt with in detail in the Needs section, some concrete needs information can be useful in the Introduction to guard against readers getting turned off by what they may consider vague ideas.

*The Capability Statement attached to this proposal details the long and successful experience of the PSO and describes the current resources of the organization.

largely ignored by existing mental health programs.

We would like to state, as our overriding concern and operating principle, that problems in living, presently identified by professionals and the public as psychological, and defined as character defects, many times stem from lack of educational, economic, and social resources, as well as from an underlying inequality between races and sexes. It is also evident to us that if communities provided supportive, comprehensive services aimed at prevention, education, and counseling in areas such as health, law, jobs, and housing, they might be able to curb the spiraling number of people who, as a last resort, are committed to or in desperation commit themselves to mental institutions, because their basic problems in living were not dealt with in their families or in the communities where they live.

There is a pressing need for alternative approaches to community mental health care, which would have as their primary focus education and prevention within the community. The purpose of a multiservice community center would be to offer a well-coordinated, central community base that would respond to a wide, yet specific range of community needs. In addition, it is hoped that such a center would bring together people with common needs and problems, and with the help of staff and coordinated resources, help them to find collective solutions and viable alternatives to their present solutions.

The major objectives of this program are:

Phrases such as "economic and social resources" can often be made stronger and more convincing by giving examples. In this case, "for example, housing, transportation, legal aid."

The definition of the *purpose* of this proposal is weak in that 1. it does not go on to say *what* the broad goal is that would be accomplished by "responding to community needs," 2. it does not say directly whether "education and prevention" referred to in the prior sentence will be offered, and 3. it does not indicate whether areas such as "health, law, jobs, and housing," referred to in the previous paragraph, would be covered. The objectives do help to clarify points 1. and 2. There is also a problem in using "education, prevention, and counseling" as if they were separate services, since education can contribute to prevention, as can counseling. Further, there is a need to be specific about what is being prevented. Is it admission or readmission to state hospitals? Is mental disorder being prevented? Some of these questions are clarified later in the proposal, but it is a mistake not to be clear as early as possible. For example, "prevention of mental illness and hospitalization" is mentioned later in objective #6. If this is the main thrust of the proposal, it should be mentioned earlier and added to the statement of purpose. Thus, the pur-

1. To help people achieve a larger measure of self-determination and to create options by providing individual and group counseling regarding legal problems, family problems, family planning, and day care, health and nutrition, education, jobs, and housing, 2. To provide a central and accessible service for the community, 3. To involve community residents in the planning and implementation of services, thereby assuring a greater degree of community involvement and control, 4. To serve as an information and referral center, and to coordinate data on existing social service agencies in the area, 5. To establish communication with and promote sharing of resources by various groups within the community such as civic and church groups, and 6. To evaluate this program as a possible model for effectiveness in the field of community mental health for the prevention of mental illness and hospitalization.

pose would read " . . . range of community needs *in order* to prevent mental illness and hospitalization."

If this is the overall purpose or goal, the *objectives* should state the strategy for achieving this goal in terms of what would be done *and* which results would be achieved. As expressed in this proposal, the objectives do indicate what would be done. However, they do not indicate what would be achieved. The objectives would be improved by adding to each one some indication of which results would be expected. For example, objective #1 might have added to it, "in order to *reduce* the extent to which these problems negatively affect people's ability to function in the family and community." Or, the following could be added, "in order to *increase* people's ability to cope with these problems of daily living." Similar phrases should be added to each objective, thereby making their connection to the prevention of mental illness and hospitalization clearer and more explicit. Doing this also presents the objectives in terms that are measurable and therefore contributes to the ability to design an evaluation of this program.

For each objective, one should ask and answer the question "what will be accomplished and will this contribute to achieving the overall purpose or goal?"

The inclusion of an evaluation objective such as #6 dictates the necessity to have a later section of the proposal on evaluation.

NEED AND RATIONALE

It was stated in the previous section of this proposal that mental health services in Plainview are failing to meet the public's needs. We would like to examine resources for this, and to present our rationale for what we believe is a viable alternative to present mental health care.

Need

It is ironic that a county which houses over one-third (approximately 19,000) of the state's mental patients is one of the most backward in the nation in terms of offering innovative and preventive mental health services. At present count, Plainview has only four county-run mental health clinics, and less than a dozen private-contract (contracted by the county) agencies to service a population of 1 million in an area of over 500 square miles. There is only one crisis-telephone hotline, and no halfway houses in the county.

Although there is no formal data available on the effectiveness of services or treatment offered in these mental health clinics, it is obvious to the participant or observer that they are grossly understaffed, that waiting lists are long, that they cater primarily to white clients with incomes well above the poverty level, and that they are staffed with white professionals (as well as a large number of foreign-born psychiatrists who have difficulty communicating with clients because of a basic inability to speak coherent English).

It helps to convey the coherence and unity of the proposal to show the linkage of one section to another as is done here in the first sentence of the Need section.

This statement would be strengthened by indicating the number served by the "four county-run clinics" and relating this number to an overall indicator of need. This would help convince the reader of the inadequacy of present services.

The word "data" is always plural; thus, it is used with the verb "are" not the verb "is."

This criticism would be more convincing if the writer had taken the time to get some figures on number of staff and number and characteristics of clients from available agency reports. Using such figures also helps establish the credibility of the proposal sponsors.

It is also apparent that these clinics are still relying on outdated and—particularly for low-income and minority people—irrelevant, modes of intervention and treatment. They are staffed with traditionally trained psychiatrists, psychologists, and social workers, whose practice is limited generally to individual, family, and group insight therapy. Piecemeal attempts are made to assist people with problems other than psychiatric, i.e., job, school, financial, and legal problems, to name a few. There is little coordination with other service agencies such as welfare, legal aid, or public-health clinics. The basic orientation is toward remedial crisis, rather than preventive programs designed to alleviate the cause preceding and underlying the crisis.

It has been our experience that people apply to these clinics in desperation and as a last resort, when problems have snowballed and assumed crisis proportions. In line with this, there is little if any outreach to the surrounding community or catchment area that the clinic supposedly serves.

Why such glaring inadequacies in the service system? We see one reason having to do with the conflict of interest between state and county over control and financing of mental health services. Another reason is that the helping professions' operating principle is based on the medical model,* in which people's problems are seen as purely psychological in origin and in manifestation. The

*The medical model views mental disturbance as disease oriented, and rooted in individual pathology.

Again, some form of documentation would strengthen the argument in this paragraph. Documentation is needed to make it more persuasive and encourage the reader to have confidence in its validity.

This is a good example of internal consistency; the proposal links up the need with the purpose (that is, prevention).

It is important always to define specialized terminology such as "medical model," as is done in footnote 8.

psychiatric profession has always been resistant to seeing mental illness in any other terms than psychological. The sad fact is that social services, and particularly mental health services, are oriented to keeping the profession constant and stable rather than to meet the needs of the people being served.

In line with our observations of the inadequacies of services, we think the following summaries of research findings amply demonstrate the need for a qualitatively different approach in the design and delivery of mental health services:

1. The roots of mental illness are in the social environment, not in the individual (Hollingshead and Redlich, Srole, Langner and Michael, Peck, Kaplan and Roman).

2. The lower the socioeconomic class, the higher the rate of mental illness (Hollingshead, report of Joint Commission of Mental Health).

3. Poverty and racism are in large part responsible for major mental health problems (Joint Commission on Mental Health).

4. Poor people are much more reluctant to seek help from psychiatric clinics (Avnet, Hollingshead).

5. Mental health clinic staff tend to treat their own kind (white, middle class) (Adams and McDonald, Broverman).

6. Mental hospitalization greatly increases during economic downturns and decreases during upturns (Brenner).

What these research findings indicate is not a justification for expansion of the existing service system,

To use global generalities, as done here, regarding psychiatric and mental-health services can discredit the proposal. Better wording might be "many members of the psychiatric profession have been resistant . . ."

This is a good demonstration of building the proposal's credibility, since it shows that the writers know the mental-health field. However, footnotes or a bibliography should accompany the text, giving the full references.

Notice also that the writers in presenting this material have gotten away from the global black-or-white generalities that characterize the earlier part of this section of the proposal.

Whenever research or other work is cited, it is good proposal writing to indicate the implications and rele-

but an entire restructuring of it. Since mental health is directly related to one's educational, economic, and social situation, we must assume a multidimensional approach to help remedy the multitude of related social factors that cause people to become "mentally ill." The one-dimensional, clinically oriented approach that views people as enclosed psychiatric entities is not a sufficient answer.

Rationale

In proposing a multiservice community center, we aim to provide a form of service that is primarily dictated by the particular conditions prevailing in the community. Any form of intervention undertaken must consider these conditions (and their effects on the individual) before effective service can be provided. What is needed is a basic orientation to social action and, ultimately, change, deemphasizing traditional clinical goals of adjustment to what is.

Three measures that we view as necessary vehicles for change are prevention, advocacy, and education. In order to realize our goals we will 1. need professionals and community people alike who are willing to act as advocates for clients first, before the needs of any particular institution or agency. We will seek out and attempt to work closely with other agencies dedicated to advocacy, such as People for Adequate Service and the Local Action Committee. 2. We need to work toward prevention of overwhelming stress situations that all too frequently result in mental hospitalization. To do this, we need to pro-

vance of these references to the program being proposed. This is skillfully handled in this paragraph.

The Need section is well done but would be more convincing with additional concrete documentation of the nature and extent of the problem.

In this sample proposal the Rationale is incorporated with the statement of Need. It could also be a separate section, or the first part of the Program section. Regardless of format, the content of the rationale should set the stage for the program description and should also serve to justify the program activities that are proposed.

When reference to cooperating agencies is made, there should be some description of them and supporting letters from these agencies.

Notice that the rationale is stressing *advocacy*. From the standpoint of internal consistency, the proposal writers should have highlighted the

vide encouragement and direct assistance in formulating specific needs, stating complaints, and asserting basic rights. 3. We need to educate people regarding their basic rights: to receive adequate public assistance, their legal options and rights, decent housing, free or low-cost quality care for children, medical care, consumer rights. 4. We need to provide a focal point within the community for residents to work together on, and receive assistance with, their basic problems in living.

We chose the community of Plainview for our pilot project because it presents the greatest need in terms of relevant social services. In comparison with the rest of the county, it has one of the highest unemployment rates and number of people receiving public assistance; one of the lowest in terms of median income and educational attainment. In addition, there is evidence of a lack of decent and sufficient housing as well as wide-scale housing discrimination. Although conclusive figures are not available, it is estimated that admission rates to state hospitals are significantly higher from this area.

We recognize that an attempt to change the present service system, and to reorder priorities of mental health care, will not happen over night. One community center will certainly not cure the ills of an entire system. We are well aware of the fact that unless the poor have some gain in their economic situation, self-sufficiency and determination will not be attained; of fundamental im-

advocacy approach in the Introduction and Need sections. The writers need to go back and consider revising the Introduction and the statements of purpose and objectives to be sure that they are consistent with the advocacy approach that is developed in this section.

The writers have introduced needs material as part of the rationale. This may be appropriate if the detailed statements documenting the high unemployment, public assistance, and other rates referred to are already presented in the Need section. In this proposal they were not included. The writers need to go back and add this material to the Need section.

This is an example of how to recognize the limitations of the proposal in a way that contributes to the proposal's credibility.

portance is basic income support for poor people.

Yet we must, at some point, begin to address people's priorities. Evidence strongly supports organizing and offering alternatives, at the community level. With a maximum amount of planning and participation by residents, a sizable contribution can be made to the mental health and well-being of the community as a whole.

PROGRAM DESIGN

To accomplish the objectives set forth in this proposal, the following coordination and program design will be implemented.

Program Development and Coordination

The first step in the coordination of the Multiservice Community Center will be the formation of a *Community Advisory Committee*. Membership will include the PSO's board of directors, leaders of civic, church, and community groups, and consumer representatives drawn from the community at large. The committee will be responsible initially for: 1. location of a suitable site for the Center; 2. promotion and publicity of the program by way of intensive mass-media publicity, and outreach to community residents and organizations; 3. establishment of program policies; 4. election of a board of directors; and 5. recommendations for hiring of staff.

The limitations are not just left standing. The writers attempt to show that in spite of the limitations the proposed program is a valuable undertaking, which will result in benefits to the community. They could have gone on to explain how, through the evaluation, the program would also contribute to developing new approaches that can be adopted in other places.

The writers again show the linkage between the objectives and the specific program activities.

Instead of stressing the area of "coordination," it would be more to the point to talk about planning and development of the "Center." It makes a proposal much clearer to list each specific program activity with separate headings, as the writers have done in this entire section. However, in doing so it is important that the headings be clear. Further, the headings in the program section should be as active as possible, so that they denote specific tasks to be done. The initial part of this section of the proposal could have been organized more effectively if there were one general heading such as "1. Program Development" and then subheadings such as:

Training and Recruitment of Staff

Staff will be recruited on the basis of experience, knowledge of, and familiarity with, the basic objectives of the center program. Staff will be recruited, to the extent possible, from the Plainview area through newspaper advertising, notices in prominent locations throughout the area, and recommendations from the advisory committee. Final selection of staff will be determined by the board of directors of PSO.

An initial training program will be instituted for new staff, and in addition, an ongoing training program will be provided for Center staff and interested community residents. The training will be directed at developing indigenous leadership and expertise within the community, both at the professional and communal levels.

Program Activities

The Center will be located in a central section of Plainview, readily accessible to railway and local bus service. It will be open six days a week, Monday through Saturday. Services will be available during both day and evening hours, and transportation will be provided to and from the Center when necessary.

Open forums will be held regularly at the Center on issues of particular interest to staff and community, such as the housing dilemma, welfare rights, employment, etc. These forums will be open to the

A. Appointment of Advisory Committee

B. Recruitment and Training of Staff

C. Location of Site

D. Establishment of Program Policies

E. Publicizing the Program

Under each of these headings there should be a narrative of the tasks that would go into the activity and the way in which these tasks would be carried out.

Since in describing these program activities it is necessary to refer to certain aspects of the overall administrative structure, it is good practice to also refer the reader to the section of the proposal where the administrative structure is described in more detail.

The program activities or services of the Center are well grouped in this part of the proposal. Their presentation would be enhanced if the writers were more direct in showing the relationship of these activities to the objectives. This can be done in two ways. First by showing which activities are related to which objectives. The writers have done some of this under ''1. Structural Group Workshops,'' in their discussion of the purpose of the workshops. However, the three purposes listed do not correspond to the way the objectives were stated in the Introduction section of the proposal.

The second way to make the connection between program activities and objectives is to explain how the activity will contribute to accomplishing the objective. The writers have accomplished this in a

community and representatives from both public and grass-roots organizations will be invited to participate.

DIRECT SERVICES

Structured Group Workshops: The purpose of these workshops is threefold: 1. to educate residents of their rights as citizens; 2. to provide support and encouragement by both group members and leaders, in exploring alternative solutions to specific problems in living; 3. to assist group members in achieving—collectively—a large measure of self-sufficiency and determination.

The workshops will be run by a professionally trained staff member, experienced in that particular area, in conjunction with one community worker who has, ideally, had experience in negotiating the particular "system" in question (courts, welfare, hospitals).

Both community worker and professional will serve as advocates for group members in naming and following out a course of action. The workshops will be small in size, numbering between six and twelve members, and will meet weekly. Workshops will be organized around the following topic areas, with the understanding that groups will be modified or expanded in accordance with the needs of residents.

Legal Assistance Workshop: Will be run by a lawyer employed by the Center whose purpose will be to inform people of the law and their legal rights. The community worker serving as coleader will accompany people to court and legal aid, and in

number of places in their discussion of the workshop activities.

Note that the word "system" so often used in the human service field has been clarified by the writers in the text by giving examples "(courts, welfare, hospitals)."

Although the series of workshops is adequately described in this proposal, the writers have not adequately described how people would be recruited, selected, and admitted into the workshops. This is a frequent omission in human service program proposals. It should be handled in a separate subsection on "recruitment and selection of participants" or "intake" or "admission to the program."

The proposal also reveals another weakness that often appears in the program section of human service proposals. That is, it does not provide summaries of the estimated number of people who will be served by each activity and in the aggregate. It also has not adequately described the characteristics of those who would be served in terms of the expected racial, sex, age, and problem backgrounds of the participants. Brief estimates of these items strengthen a proposal, since they convey careful planning and understanding of the program to the funder.

general, act as an advocate for that group member.

Employment Workshop: Will provide counseling regarding 1. careers: helping people decide what field to enter; 2. reentry: helping older people, or those who have been out of work for a long period, to get back into the labor force; 3. job rights: teaching people what their employment rights are under the law; how to fight job discrimination when it occurs; procedures for unionizing; where to get specific job training.

Education Workshop: To assist those interested in further education to 1. identify and evaluate the skills they already have developed—either through life experience or jobs; 2. to explore available schools and educational programs and help choose those that best meet the person's needs.

Welfare/Public Assistance Workshop: To educate in regard to welfare rights; to inform of eligibility requirements and regulations of DSS, SSI, Medicaid, and social security; to directly assist in negotiating and receiving these services.

Health and Nutrition: To be run by a registered nurse, employed by the Center, and community worker. Purpose will be to discuss basic health needs and preventive measures, correct diet, and nutrition; and to identify what conditions warrant medical attention. When necessary, direct referrals will be made to the Plainview West Health Center and to the Plainview East Community Health Center.

Housing: Purpose will be 1. to di-

Note an inconsistency in the titling of these activities. Each of the prior activities included the word workshop in the heading. The writers, perhaps in order not to be repetitive, have dropped that word. This inconsistency can raise a question for the reader of whether or not we are still talking about "workshops."

rectly assist people in securing safe, comfortable and low-cost housing; 2. to inform people of their rights as tenants; 3. to assist people when faced with housing discrimination; 4. to work in conjunction with other agencies such as Council of Churches Housing Bureau and the local action committee on issues and problems pertaining to housing.

Family Problems: This group(s) will focus on specific marital problems such as separation and divorce, and examine issues relating to sex roles, the single parent, family planning, and day care.

In addition to these workshops, there will be crisis intervention, through both group and individual counseling. The primary purpose of this service will be 1. to offer support to persons who are suicidal and/or who are undergoing enormous stress due to death of a loved one, overuse of drugs or alcohol, loss of job, failure in school or work, serious physical illness, etc.; 2. to help find an immediate short-term solution to the presenting problem, and 3. to prevent, whenever possible, hospitalization.

The writers are now describing a different type of program activity—"crisis intervention"—which is not a workshop. A new subheading should be used to emphasize that this is another activity.

A child-care service, run by two community aides, will be provided for residents attending the Center. Referrals will be made to Plainview Head Start and Day-Care Center for those needing extended day-care services.

Here is an example of another activity buried in the text. It should be highlighted by using the subheading "Child-Care Services."

REFERRAL SERVICES
The Center will organize and maintain an extensive *Data Bank* for referral services and information concerning jobs, housing, legal services,

transportation, schools, consumer information, etc. The entire staff will be responsible for the maintenance and updating of the information and services contained in the bank. Residents referred to other community or service agencies will be urged to give the staff feedback (by way of phone call or short questionnaire) on the agency's responsiveness (or lack of it) to the resident.

Screening of services named in the bank will be an ongoing staff activity. In the initial stages of the program, a representative of the staff will be delegated to visit each agency in the area to determine the nature of and assist the effectiveness of that agency or program.

Coordination with Other Agencies

One of the stated objectives of the program is to promote the sharing of resources and to avoid unnecessary duplication of services. In addition to the regularly held forums, one or two representatives from other agencies within the area will be invited each month to open "community meetings," held at the Center. Initially, these meetings will serve to inform other agencies of our services and activities. The overall, and continuing, purpose of these meetings will be to discuss ways in which collectively we can be more responsive to the needs of the community. Open invitations will be extended to local civic groups and church groups in addition to service agencies.

Here, the writers have successfully made explicit the linkage between a program activity and an objective.

This shows the reader that the proposal writers have a knowledge of how to implement this activity. Giving an indication of the number of

Program Evaluation

As the Multiservice Community Center is to serve as a model program for other communities, a major aspect of its design will be program evaluation. A detailed research design will be developed and implemented in cooperation with the funding agency in the beginning stages of the program. Progress reports will be made regularly.

Briefly stated here, the evaluation will take into account: 1. Utilization of Center services: who attends the Center, how often, under what circumstances, 2. Assessment of residents' attitudes toward and opinions of services, 3. Success in meeting primary goals and objectives, 4. Number of admissions to state hospitals from the Plainview area before and after establishment of the Center, 5. Measurable change within the community, 6. Impact of program on other community agencies.

ADMINISTRATION AND STAFFING

Community Advisory Committee

The Community Advisory Committee will be made up of individuals selected from the PSO Board of Directors, civic, church, and community leaders from within the Plainview community, and community rep-

groups in the community that would be invited would make this even more convincing.

It is evident that there is not a design for evaluation of the program. The writers are, in effect, saying that they recognize a need for an evaluation but would like to design it later. This may be acceptable to some funders, but it is advisable to clear this with the funding agency before submitting the complete proposal. Many funders would expect a more detailed statement of the evaluation.

The composition and responsibilities of all committees and boards. This is pointed out in this proposal but it would also be helpful to indicate the number of people who would be on the committee; and, if

resentatives. The Community Advisory Committee will be responsible for making suggestions and recommendations to the Center Board of Directors on matters of program development and services, and act as a liaison between the community and Center to assure increased sensitivity toward the community it serves.

Board of Directors

The existing PSO Board of Directors will act as the primary policy and decision-making body to reflect the needs and scope of the Center as seen by the Community Advisory Committee. The board will meet once a month, and membership will encompass a wide range of business, mental health, legal, and community (both professional and civic) representation from Suffolk County.

The board will be directly responsible for insuring that the Center is continually providing high-quality services; that responsible personnel are staffing the Center, and directing their energies to programs that the community wants. The board of directors is the overseer and coordinator of the Center *for the community*. The executive director of the Center will report directly to the board on a monthly basis. The board of directors is also responsible for the maintenance of sound fiscal and personnel policies. Areas involving general responsibilities of the Center, especially on internal bases such as personnel and financial matters, will

possible, to list their names and positions.

A list of this existing board could be included in the capability statement that will accompany this proposal.

be handled by committees which will report directly to the board.

Executive Director

The Center director will be responsible for the overall running and day-to-day activities of the program. (S)he will have the major responsibility for the content, direction, and implementation of Center services, as put forth by the board of directors.

The director will sit on committees set up to coordinate finance, public relations, and personnel, and will report monthly to the board of directors. In addition, the director will work in conjunction with, and delegate responsibility to, two staff coordinators, for the supervision and training of staff.

QUALIFICATIONS:
The position will call for training and experience in the clinical, planning, and community organization aspects of social service delivery.

Staff Coordinators:

Two full-time positions. Responsible for working in a supervisory and training capacity in conjunction with the executive director; in charge of organizing and overseeing the direct-service workshops, referral service, and coordination with other agencies. Will also participate in

An organizational chart similar to the example shown in Figure 3 would help to clarify the board, committee, and staff structure that is being proposed.

For positions of major responsibility such as executive directors, a more specific statement of qualifications should be included, explaining minimum education and experience that will be accepted. Such as: "advanced degree in social welfare" and "3–5 years experience in administration of social agencies."

leading the education, housing, employment, and welfare workshops.

QUALIFICATIONS:
MSW, and minimum of five years' experience in community mental health services; thorough knowledge of the social service agency network.

The writers have, for the positions, provided the specificity they failed to include for other positions.

Psychiatrist:

One part-time position. Responsible for heading crisis-intervention workshop and individual counseling; making psychiatric evaluations, and prescribing and dispensing drugs when necessary. In addition, will participate in training of staff.

QUALIFICATIONS:
Position will call for experience with community mental health delivery, both community-clinic and -hospital aspects.

Where part-time positions are indicated, the amount of time should be explained, for example, "one half-time" or "100 days."

Psychologist:

One full-time position: will be responsible for running family workshop and share responsibility with the psychiatrist for evaluation and crisis-intervention counseling.

QUALIFICATIONS:
Training and experience in family counseling and child psychology.

Lawyer:

One part-time position; responsible for running legal workshop and consulting with staff on all legal matters.

QUALIFICATIONS:
Legal experience with economic problems, family problems, landlord–tenant problems, and criminal matters. Candidate with job experience in community legal-services agency preferred.

Nurse:

One full-time RN to run health and nutrition workshop, make referrals to appropriate agencies, such as health clinics and hospitals, and provide individual counseling on matters of health and nutrition.

QUALIFICATIONS:
Extensive experience in public health nursing.

Community Workers:

Two full-time positions for local residents. Responsibilities will include: acting as coleaders for direct service workshops; serving as liaison between clients and staff; acting as advocates for clients; making referrals for clients to other agencies when necessary; participating in outreach efforts to inform residents of the programs being offered.

Child-Care Worker:

Two part-time positions for community residents. Duties will include the supervision and care of children of clients attending the Center.

Bus Driver:

One full-time position; responsible for transporting residents to and from the Center and, when necessary, to other agencies.

Secretary:

Two full-time positions. Duties will include: obtaining intake information on new clients; referring clients to appropriate services or staff within the Center; maintaining files, data bank, and correspondence; taking minutes at Center meetings.

Receptionist:

One full-time position. Responsibilities will be to cover the telephones and to schedule appointments for clients.

In proposals with a fairly large staff complement, it helps to clarify the staffing pattern to include a summary chart that shows each job title, the number of people, and the level of effort (this is, amount of time). An example of such a summary chart for this proposal is shown in Table 4.

Table 4.
Summary of Staffing Pattern

POSITION	# OF PEOPLE	LEVEL OF EFFORT
Executive Director	1	full time
Staff Coordinator	2	full time
Psychiatrist	1	half time
Psychologist	1	full time
Lawyer	1	half time
Nurse	1	full time
Community Workers	2	full time
Child-Care Workers	2	half time
Bus Driver	1	full time
Secretary	2	full time
Receptionist	1	full time

Appendix B: Foundation Center Libraries

The following is a listing of the Foundation Center's Cooperating Library Collections in each state. To obtain information on changes and new locations, telephone toll free 800-424-9836.

Alabama
Birmingham Public Library
2020 Park Place
Birmingham 35203
205-254-2541

Auburn University at
  Montgomery Library
Montgomery 36193
205-279-9110

Alaska
University of Alaska,
  Anchorage Library
3211 Providence Drive
Anchorage 99504
907-263-1848

Arizona
Phoenix Public Library
Social Sciences Subject
  Department
12 East McDowell Road
Phoenix 85004
602-262-4782

Tucson Public Library
Main Library
200 South Sixth Avenue
Tucson 85701
602-791-4393

Arkansas

Westark Community College
    Library
Grand Avenue at Waldron Rd.
Fort Smith 72913
501-785-4241

Little Rock Public Library
Reference Department
700 Louisiana Street
Little Rock 72201
501-374-7546

California

California Community
    Foundation
1644 Wilshire Boulevard
Los Angeles 90017
213-413-4042

San Diego Public Library
820 E Street
San Diego 92101
714-236-5816

Santa Barbara Public Library
Reference Section
40 East Anapamu
P.O. Box 1019
Santa Barbara 93102
805-962-7653

Colorado

Denver Public Library
Sociology Division
1357 Broadway
Denver 80203
303-573-5152

Connecticut

Hartford Public Library
Reference Department
500 Main Street
Hartford 06103
203-525-9121

Delaware

Hugh Morris Library
University of Delaware
Newark 19711
302-738-2965

Florida

Jacksonville Public Library
Business, Science, and
    Industry Department
122 North Ocean Street
Jacksonville 32202
904-633-3926

Miami—Dade Public Library
Florida Collection
One Biscayne Boulevard
Miami 33132
305-579-5001

Georgia

Atlanta Public Library
1 Margaret Mitchell Square at
    Forsyth and Carnegie Way
Atlanta 30303
404-688-4636

Hawaii

Thomas Hale Hamilton Library
University of Hawaii
Humanities and Social
    Sciences Division
2550 The Mall
Honolulu 96822
808-948-7214

Idaho

Caldwell Public Library
1010 Dearborn Street
Caldwell 83605
208-459-3242

Illinois

Donors Forum of Chicago
208 South LaSalle Street
Chicago 60604
312-726-4882

Sangamon State University
    Library
Shepherd Road
Springfield 62708
217-786-6633

Indiana

Indianapolis—Marion County
    Public Library
40 East St. Clair Street
Indianapolis 46204
317-269-1733

Iowa
Public Library of Des Moines
100 Locust Street
Des Moines 50309
515-283-4259

Kansas
Topeka Public Library
Adult Services Department
1515 West Tenth Street
Topeka 66604
913-233-2040

Kentucky
Louisville Free Public Library
Fourth and York Streets
Louisville 40203
502-584-4154

Louisiana
East Baton Rouge Parish Library
Centroplex Library
120 St. Louis Street
Baton Rouge 70802
504-344-5291

New Orleans Public Library
Business and Science Division
219 Loyola Avenue
New Orleans 70140
504-586-4919

Maine
University of Southern Maine
Center for Research and
    Advanced Study
246 Deering Avenue
Portland 04102
207-780-4411

Maryland
Enoch Pratt Free Library
Social Science and History
    Department
400 Cathedral Street
Baltimore 21201
301-396-5320

Massachusetts
Associated Grantmakers of
    Massachusetts
294 Washington Street

Suite 501
Boston 02108
617-426-2608

Boston Public Library
Copley Square
Boston 02117
617-536-5400

Michigan
Alpena County Library
211 North First Avenue
Alpena 49707
517-356-6188

Henry Ford Centennial Library
16301 Michigan Avenue
Dearborn 48126
313-943-2337

Purdy Library
Wayne State University
Detroit 48202
313-577-4040

Michigan State Univeristy
    Libraries
Reference Library
East Lansing 48824
517-353-8816

University of Michigan—Flint
UM—F Library
Reference Department
Flint 48503
313-762-3408

Grand Rapids Public Library
Sociology and Education Dept.
Library Plaza
Grand Rapids 49502
616-456-4411

Michigan Technological
    University Library
Highway U.S. 41
Houghton 49931
906-487-2507

Minnesota
Minneapolis Public Library
Sociology Department
300 Nicollet Mall
Minneapolis 55401
612-372-6555

Mississippi
Jackson Metropolitan Library
301 North State Street
Jackson 39201
601-944-1120

Missouri
Clearinghouse for Midcontinent
 Foundations
Univ. of Missouri, Kansas City
Law School, Suite 1–300
52nd Street and Oak
Kansas City 64113
816-276-1176

Kansas City Public Library
311 East 12th Street
Kansas City 64106
816-221-2685

Metropolitan Association for
 Philanthropy, Inc.
5600 Oakland, G-324
St. Louis 63110
314-647-2290

Springfield—Greene County
 Library
397 East Central Street
Springfield 65801
417-869-4621

Montana
Eastern Montana College
 Library
Reference Department
Billings 59101
406-657-2337

Nebraska
W. Dale Clark Library
Social Sciences Department
215 South 15th Street
Omaha 68102
402-444-4822

Nevada
Clark County Library
1401 East Flamingo Road
Las Vegas 89109
702-733-7810

Washoe County Library
301 South Center Street
Reno 89505
702-785-4190

New Hampshire
The New Hampshire Charitable
 Fund
One South Street
P.O. Box 1335
Concord 03301
603-225-6641

New Jersey
New Jersey State Library
Governmental Reference
185 West State Street
P.O. Box 1898
Trenton 08625
609-292-6220

New Mexico
New Mexico State Library
300 Don Gaspar Street
Santa Fe 87501
505-827-2033

New York
New York State Library
Cultural Education Center
Humanities Section
Empire State Plaza
Albany 12230
518-474-7645

Buffalo and Erie County
 Public Library
Lafayette Square
Buffalo 14203
716-856-7525

Levittown Public Library
Reference Department
One Bluegrass Lane
Levittown 11756
516-731-5728

Plattsburgh Public Library
Reference Department
15 Oak Street
Plattsburgh 12901
518-563-0921

Rochester Public Library
Business and Social Sciences
    Division
115 South Avenue
Rochester 14604
716-428-7328

Onondaga County Public Library
335 Montgomery Street
Syracuse 13202
315-473-4491

North Carolina
North Carolina State Library
109 East Jones Street
Raleigh 27611
919-733-3270

The Winston-Salem Foundation
229 First Union National Bank
    Building
Winston-Salem 27101
919-725-2382

North Dakota
The Library
North Dakota State University
Fargo 58105
701-237-8876

Ohio
Public Library of Cincinnati and
    Hamilton County
Education Department
800 Vine Street
Cincinnati 45202
513-369-6940

Toledo-Lucas County Public
    Library
Social Science Department
325 Michigan Street
Toledo 43624
419-255-7055 ext. 221

Oklahoma
Oklahoma City Community
    Foundation
1300 North Broadway
Oklahoma City 73103
405-235-5621

Tulsa City-County Library System
400 Civic Center
Tulsa 74103
918-581-5144

Oregon
Library Association of Portland
Education and Documents Rm.
801 S.W. Tenth Avenue
Portland 97205
503-223-7201

Pennsylvania
The Free Library of Philadelphia
Logan Square
Philadelphia 19103
215-686-5423

Hillman Library
University of Pittsburgh
Pittsburgh 15260
412-624-4528

Rhode Island
Providence Public Library
Reference Department
150 Empire Street
Providence 02903
401-521-7722

South Carolina
South Carolina State Library
Reader Services Department
1500 Senate Street
Columbia 29211
803-758-3181

South Dakota
South Dakota State Library
State Library Building
322 South Fort Street
Pierre 57501
605-773-3131

Tennessee
Resources Center for Non-Profit
    Agencies, Inc.
502 Gay Street, Suite 201
P.O. Box 1606
Knoxville 37901
615-521-6034

Memphis Public Library
1850 Peabody Avenue
Memphis 38104
901-528-2957

Texas
The Hogg Foundation for Mental
    Health
The University of Texas
Austin 78712
512-471-5041

Corpus Christi State University
    Library
6300 Ocean Drive
Corpus Christi 78412
512-991-6810

Dallas Public Library
Grants Information Service
1954 Commerce Street
Dallas 75201
214-748-9071 ext. 332

El Paso Community Foundation
El Paso National Bank Building
Suite 1616
El Paso 79901
915-533-4020

Houston Public Library
Bibliographic & Information Center
500 McKinney Avenue
Houston 77002
713-224-5441 ext. 265

Funding Information Library
Minnie Stevens Piper Foundation
201 North St. Mary's Street
Suite 100
San Antonio 78205
512-227-4333

Utah
Salt Lake City Public Library
Information and Adult Services
209 East Fifth South
Salt Lake City 84111
801-363-5733

Vermont
State of Vermont Department of
    Libraries
Reference Services Unit
111 State Street
Montpelier 05602
802-828-3261

Virginia
Grants Resources Library
Ninth Floor
Hampton City Hall
Hampton 23669
804-727-6496

Richmond Public Library
Business, Science, & Technology
    Department
101 East Franklin Street
Richmond 23219
804-780-8223

Washington
Seattle Public Library
1000 Fourth Avenue
Seattle 98104
206-625-4881

Spokane Public Library
Reference Department
West 906 Main Avenue
Spokane 99201
509-838-3361

West Virginia
Kanawha County Public Library
123 Capitol Street
Charleston 25301
304-343-4646

Wisconsin
Marquette University Memorial
    Library
1415 West Wisconsin Avenue
Milwaukee 53233
414-224-1515

Wyoming
Laramie County Community
    College Library
1400 East College Drive
Cheyenne 82001
307-634-5853

Canada
The Canadian Centre for Philanthropy
12 Sheppard Street, 3rd Floor
Toronto, Ontario M5H 3A1
416-364-4875

Mexico
Biblioteca Benjamin Franklin
Londres 16
Mexico City 6, D.F.

Puerto Rico
Consumer Education and Service
    Center
Department of Consumer Affairs
Minillas Central Government
    Building North
Santurce 00904

Virgin Islands
College of the Virgin Islands Library
Saint Thomas
U.S. Virgin Islands 00801
809-774-1252

Appendix C: State Foundation Guides

There are a number of directories and guides that identify foundations in particular states. A bibliography of these directories has been compiled by Jo Alyce Newgaard, librarian of the Foundation Center. The Foundation Center bibliography reviews the following:*

Alabama (184 foundations). *Alabama Foundation Directory.* Edited by Anne F. Knight. 1980. 25 p. Based primarily on 1978 990-PF and 990-AR returns filed with the IRS. Main section arranged alphabetically by foundation. Indexes of geographic areas and major areas of interest. Available from Birmingham Public Library, 2020 Park Place, Birmingham, Alabama 35203. $5.00 prepaid.

California (439 foundations). *Guide to California Foundations.* 2nd edition. Prepared by the San Francisco Study Center. 1978. vii, 294 p. Based primarily on 1976 and 1977 990-PF and 990-AR returns filed with the IRS or records in the California Attorney General's Office. Some additional data supplied by foundations completing questionnaires. Main section arranged alphabetically by foundation. Index of foundation names for all foundations in directory; indexes of primary interests and geographic area only for those foundations which completed questionnaires; index of community foundations. Available from Guide to Cali-

---

*Jo Alyce Newgaard, *Bibliography of Area Foundation Directories,* February 1981. Reprinted with permission of The Foundation Center, New York, N.Y. Only included here are the directories published since 1976.

fornia Foundations, P.O. Box 5646, San Francisco, California 94101.
Make check or money order payable to: Northern California Foundations
Group. $6.00 prepaid.

California (73 foundations). *San Diego County Foundation Directory 1980.* Compiled by The Community Congress of San Diego, Inc.
1980. 72 p. Based on 1977–1979 CT-2 forms filed with the California
Attorney-General's Office. Available from Community Congress of San
Diego, 1172 Morena Boulevard, San Diego, California 92110. $10.00
prepaid.

California (45 Bay Area foundations). *Small Change from Big
Bucks: A Report and Recommendations on Bay Area Foundations and
Social Change.* Edited by Herb Allen and Sam Sternberg. 1979. 226 p.
Based primarily on 1976 990-AR returns filed with the IRS, CT-2 forms
filed with California, annual reports, and interviews with foundations.
Available from Bay Area Committee for Responsive Philanthropy, 944
Market Street, San Francisco, California 94102. Make check payable to:
Regional Young Adult Project. $6.00 prepaid.

California (525 foundations). *Where the Money's At, How to
Reach Over 500 California Grant-Making Foundations.* Edited by
Patricia Blair Tobey with Irving R. Warner as Contributing Editor. 1978.
536 p. Based on 1975 to 1977 (mainly 1976) California CT-2 forms in
the California Registry of Charitable Trusts office. Main section arranged
alphabetically by foundation. Indexes of foundation name, foundation
name within either Northern or Southern California, county, and foundation personnel. Available from ICPR Publications, 9255 Sunset Boulevard, 8th Floor, Los Angeles, California 90069. $17.00

Colorado (approximately 192 foundations). *Colorado Foundation
Directory.* 2nd edition. Co-sponsored by the Junior League of Denver,
Inc., the Denver Foundation, and the Attorney General of Colorado.
1980. 61 p. Based on 1977 through 1979 (mostly 1978) 990-PF and 990-
AR returns filed with the IRS and information supplied by foundations.
Main section arranged alphabetically by foundation. Also sections on
proposal writing, sample proposal, and sample budget form. Appendixes
of foundations by assets, grants, and fields of interest, and bibliography.
Available from Colorado Foundation Directory, Junior League of Denver, Inc., 1805 South Bellaire, Suite 400, Denver, Colorado 80222. Make
check payable to: Colorado Foundation Directory. $7.00 prepaid.

Connecticut (590 foundations). *A Directory of Foundations in the
State of Connecticut.* 3rd edition. Edited by John Parker Huber. 1976. xv,
168 p. Based on 1973 990-PF and 990-AR returns filed with the IRS.
Available from Eastern Connecticut State College Foundation, Inc.,

P.O. Box 431, Willimantic, Connecticut 06226. $7.00 prepaid; otherwise $8.00.

Connecticut (approximately 465 foundations). *1979 Connecticut Foundation Directory*. Edited by Michael E. Burns. 1979. 92 p. Based primarily on 1977 and 1978 990-PF and 990-AR returns filed with the IRS. Main section arranged alphabetically by foundation. Available from DATA, 1 State Street, New Haven, Connecticut 06511. $10 prepaid.

Delaware (558 foundations). *Delaware Foundations*. Compiled by United Way of Delaware, Inc. 1979. viii, 116 p. Based on 1976 through 1978 990-PF and 990-AR returns filed with the IRS, annual reports, and information supplied by foundations. Main section arranged alphabetically by foundation. Includes 96 private foundations, a sampling of company-sponsored foundations and corporate giving programs, 24 operating foundations, and 438 out-of-state foundations. Available from United Way of Delaware, Inc., 701 Shipley Street, Wilmington, Delaware 19801. $7.50 prepaid.

District of Columbia (approximately 500 foundations). *The Washington D.C. Metropolitan Area Foundation Directory*. Edited by Julia Mills Jacobsen and Kay Carter Courtade. 1979. 80 p. Based on 1976 and 1977 990-PF and 990-AR returns filed with the IRS and information supplied by foundations. Main section arranged alphabetically by foundations; also sections listing nongrantmaking foundations, operating foundations, inactive foundations, and dissolved foundations. Indexes of foundation names and of officers and trustees. Available from Management Communications, Publications Division, 4416 Edmunds Street, N.W., Washington, D.C. 20007. $13.50.

Georgia (approximately 550 foundations). *Georgia Foundation Directory*. Compiled by Ann Bush. 1979. 28 p. Based on 1976 through 1978 990-PF and 990-AR returns filed with the IRS. Foundation addresses not included. No indexes. Available from Foundation Collection, Atlanta Public Library, 10 Pryor Street, S.W., Atlanta, Georgia 30303. Free.

Georgia (530 foundations). *Guide to Foundations in Georgia*. Compiled by the Georgia Department of Human Resources. 1978. xv, 145 p. Based on 1975 through 1977 990-PF and 990-AR returns filed with the IRS. Main section arranged alphabetically by foundation. Indexes of foundation names, cities, and program interests. Available from State Economic Opportunity Unit, Office of District Programs, Department of Human Resources, 618 Ponce de Leon Avenue, N.E., Atlanta, Georgia 30308. Free.

Idaho (78 foundations). *Directory of Idaho Foundations*. 2nd edition. Prepared by the Caldwell Public Library. 1980. 12 p. Based on mostly 1978 and 1979 990-PF and 990-AR returns filed with the IRS. Main section arranged alphabetically by foundation. Available from The Foundation Collection, Caldwell Public Library, 1010 Dearborn Street, Caldwell, Idaho 83605. $1.00 prepaid and $.28 in postage stamps.

Illinois (approximately 1900 foundations). *Illinois Foundation Directory*. Edited by Beatrice J. Capriotti and Frank J. Capriotti III. 1978. ix, 527 p., various additional pagings. Based on mostly 1976 and 1977 990-PF and 990-AR returns filed with the IRS plus correspondence with some foundations. Main section arranged alphabetically by foundation. Table of contents alphabetical by foundation name. No indexes. Available from the Foundation Data Center, 100 Wesley Temple Building, 123 East Grant Street, Minneapolis, Minnesota 55403. $425.

Indiana (265 foundations). *Indiana Foundations: A Directory*. Edited by Paula Reading Spear. 1979. iii, 175 p. Based on 1977 through 1979 (mostly 1978) 990-PF and 990-AR returns filed with the IRS and information supplied by foundations. Main section arranged alphabetically by foundation. Indexes of financial criteria, subject, and county. Appendixes of restricted foundations, foundations for student assistance only, and dissolved foundations. Available from Central Research Systems, 320 North Meridian, Suite 1011, Indianapolis, Indiana 46204. $19.95 prepaid.

Kansas (approximately 255 foundations). *Directory of Kansas Foundations*. Edited by Connie Townsley. 1979. 128 p. Based on 990-PF and 990-AR returns filed with the IRS. Fiscal date of information not provided. Main section arranged alphabetically by foundation. Index by city. Available from Association of Community Arts Councils of Kansas, Columbian Building, 4th floor, 112 West 6th, Topeka, Kansas 66603. $5.80 prepaid.

Maine (139 foundations). *A Directory of Foundations in the State of Maine*. 3rd edition. Compiled by the Center for Research and Advanced Study. 1980. ii, 59 p. Based on 1979 and 1980 990-PF and 990-AR returns filed with the IRS. Main section arranged alphabetically by city location of foundation. Also sections on basic elements in a letter of inquiry, a bibliography, a description of IRS information returns, a sample report to funding source, and a list of recent grants. Index of subjects. Available from Center for Research and Advanced Study, University of Southern Maine, 246 Deering Avenue, Portland, Maine 04102. $3.00 prepaid.

Maryland (approximately 300 foundations). *1979 Annual Index Foundation Reports*. Compiled by the Office of the Attorney General. 1980. 38 p. Based on 1979 990-PF and 990-AR returns received by the Maryland State Attorney General's Office. Main section arranged alphabetically by foundation. Includes address, principal manager, and assets. No indexes. Available from the Office of the Attorney General, One South Calvert Street, Baltimore, Maryland 21202. Attention: Sharon Smith. $5.00 prepaid.

Maryland (approximately 300 foundations). *1979 Supplemental Information Index: to the Annual Index Foundation Reports*. Compiled by the Office of the Attorney General. 1980. 142 p. Based on 1979 990-PF and 990-AR returns received by the Maryland State Attorney General's Office. Main section arranged alphabetically by foundation. Includes foundation managers and addresses, purpose, grants list, and amount approved for future payment. No indexes. Available from the Office of the Attorney General, One South Calvert Street, Baltimore, Maryland 21202. $30 prepaid.

Massachusetts (533 foundations). *Community Grants Resource Catalogue: A Directory of Philanthropic Foundations in the Commonwealth of Massachusetts*. Prepared by Steve Rubin and edited by Don Levitan. 1977. 82 p., appendixes. Based on 1973 900-PF and 990-AR returns filed with the IRS. Main section arranged alphabetically by foundation. Index of subjects. Available from Government Research Publications, Box 122, Newton Centre, Massachusetts 02159. $9.00.

Massachusetts (726 foundations). *Directory of Foundations in Massachusetts*. 1977. 135 p. Based on 1975 900-PF and 990-AR returns filed with the IRS. Prepared by Office of the Attorney-General of the Commonwealth of Massachusetts and the Associated Foundations of Greater Boston. Main section arranged in two parts—foundations which make grants primarily to organizations, and foundations which make grants primarily to individuals. Appendixes of grant amounts, geographic restrictions, purposes, loans, non-scholarship loans, scholarships-restricted by city, scholarships-population groups, and scholarships-purpose restricted. Available from University of Massachusetts Press, Box 29, Amherst, Massachusetts 01002. $7.50 prepaid.

Michigan (863 foundations). *The Michigan Foundation Directory*. 3rd edition. Prepared by the Council of Michigan Foundations and Michigan League for Human Services. 1980. vii, 113 p. Based on information compiled from foundations, the Foundation Center, and primarily 1978 tax returns filed with the IRS. Main section arranged in three parts: Section I is mainly an alphabetical listing of 304 Michigan foundations having assets of $200,000 or making annual grants of at least

$25,000; also includes brief information on 774 foundations making grants of $1,000 or more annually, geographical listing of foundations by city, terminated foundations, and special purpose foundations; Section II is a survey of Michigan foundation philanthropy; and Section III provides information for seeking grants. Indexes of subject/area of interest; donor, trustee, officer; and by foundation name. Available from Michigan League for Human Services, 200 Mill Street, Lansing, Michigan 48933. $9.00 prepaid.

Minnesota (450 foundations). *Guide to Minnesota Foundations.* 2nd edition. Prepared by the Minnesota Council on Foundations. 1980. vii, 95 p. Based on mostly 1978 and 1979 990-PF and 990-AR returns filed with the IRS and data from cooperating foundations. Main section arranged alphabetically by foundation. Covers foundations with grant totals of $25,000 or more per year, including assets, grants and major areas of interest. Also sections on smaller foundations, proposal writing, and the foundation review process. Index of foundation names. Available from Minnesota Council on Foundations, 413 Foshay Tower, Minneapolis, Minnesota 55402. $10.00 plus $.40 sales tax or your sales tax exempt number.

Nebraska (approximately 154 foundations). *Nebraska Foundation Directory.* Compiled by the Junior League of Omaha. 1979. 77 p. Based on mostly 1976 and 1977 990-PF and 990-AR returns filed with the IRS. Main section arranged alphabetically by foundation. No indexes. Available from Junior League of Omaha, 7365 Pacific Street, Omaha, Nebraska 68114. Free, limited supply.

New Hampshire (approximately 400 foundations). *Directory of Charitable Funds in New Hampshire.* 3rd edition. June 1976. 107 p. Based on 1974–1975 records in the New Hampshire Attorney-General's Office. Main section arranged alphabetically by foundation. Indexes of geographical areas when restricted, and of purposes when not geographically restricted. Available from the Office of the Attorney-General, State House Annex, Concord, New Hampshire 03301. $2.00. Annual supplement, which includes changes, deletions, and additions, available from same address for $1.00.

New Jersey (783 foundations). *Foundations in New Jersey: A Directory.* 2nd edition. Compiled by the Governmental Reference Office, Bureau of Law, Legislative and General Reference Services Division of the New Jersey State Library, Archives and History. June 1978. Irregular paging. Based on 1976 and 1977 990-PF and 990-AR returns filed with the IRS. Contains two sections: I. Alphabetical listing by foundation name with IRS number and county, and II. County listing by foundation name with address. Available from the Governmental Reference Office, New

Jersey State Library, P.O. Box 1898, Trenton, New Jersey 08625. Free; limited supply.

New Jersey (321 foundations and 374 corporations). *The New Jersey Mitchell Guide: Foundations, Corporations, and Their Managers.* 2nd edition (revised edition of *A Directory of New Jersey Foundations*). Edited by Janet A. Mitchell. 1980. vi, 218 p. Based on 1977 and 1978 990-PF and 990-AR returns filed with the IRS and information supplied by foundations. Main section arranged alphabetically by foundation. Also sections on corporations and scholarship foundations. Indexes of foundations and corporations by county and by managers. Appendixes of foundation statistics, foundations with assets over $1 million, and foundations with grant totals over $100,000. Available from The Mitchell Guides, P.O. Box 413, Princeton, New Jersey 08540. $20 prepaid.

New York (approximately 139 organizations). *Guide to Grantmakers: Rochester Area.* Compiled by the Monroe County Library System. 1980. vii, 1030 p. Based on contact with organizations and 1977 through 1980 (mostly 1979) 990-PF and 990-AR returns filed with the IRS. Main section arranged alphabetically by organization, including foundations, corporations, associations, nonprofit organizations, and individuals offering funds, services, or products. Published by Urban Information Center, Monroe County Library System, not available for purchase. May be used in libraries of Monroe County Library System and at Foundation Center Library, New York.

New York (185 foundations, 182 businesses, and 42 parent corporations). *The Long Island Mitchell Guide: Foundations, Corporations, and Their Managers.* Edited by Janet A. Mitchell. 1980. vii, 119 p. Based on mostly 1978 and 1979 990-PF and 990-AR returns filed with the IRS by foundations on Long Island and in Brooklyn and Queens. Main section arranged alphabetically by foundation. Also sections on businesses and their parent corporations. Indexes of foundations and corporations by name and by managers. Appendixes of foundation statistics, foundations with assets over $500,000, and foundations with grant totals over $50,000. Available from The Mitchell Guides, P.O. Box 413, Princeton, New Jersey 08540. $20 prepaid.

New York (950 entries). *New York Foundation Profiles.* Edited by James H. Taylor. 1976. 259 p. Based on 1974 and 1975 990-PF and 990-AR returns filed with the IRS. Main section arranged alphabetically by foundation. Index of foundations. Available from Davis-Taylor Associates, Inc., Route 3, Box 289, Mt. Morgan Road, Williamsburg, Kentucky 40769. $29.95.

New York (323 foundations, 362 businesses, and 88 parent corporations). *The Upstate New York Mitchell Guide: Foundations, Corporations, and Their Managers.* Edited by Janet A. Mitchell, 1980. vii, 216 p. Based on mostly 1978 990-PF and 990-AR returns filed with the IRS by foundations in upstate New York and Westchester County. Main section arranged alphabetically by foundation. Also sections on businesses and their parent corporations. Indexes of foundations and corporations by regions and by managers. Appendixes of foundation statistics, foundations with assets over $1 million, and foundations with grant totals over $100,000. Available from The Mitchell Guides, P.O. Box 413, Princeton, New Jersey 08540. $25.00 prepaid.

North Carolina (415 foundations). *A Guide to Foundations of the Southeast.* Volume II: North Carolina, South Carolina. Edited by Jerry C. Davis. 1975. x, 200 p. Based on 1973 and 1974 990-PF and 990-AR returns filed with the IRS. Main section arranged alphabetically by foundation within each state. Index of officers. Published by Davis-Taylor Associates, Inc., out of print.

Ohio (3500 foundations). *Charitable Foundations Directory of Ohio.* 3rd edition. 1978. 185 p. Based on 1973 to 1977 records in the Ohio Attorney-General's Office and returns filed with the IRS. Includes information on all charitable organizations reporting to the Attorney-General under Ohio Revised Code 109.31 and the Federal Tax Reform Act of 1969 (trusts, foundations, charitable organizations). Main section arranged alphabetically by foundation. Indexes of counties, purposes, and foundation names. Available from Charitable Foundations Directory, Attorney-General's Office, 30 East Broad Street, 15th Floor, Columbus, Ohio 43215. $4.00 prepaid.

Oregon (282 foundations). *The Guide to Oregon Foundations.* Produced by the Tri-County Community Council, a United Way Agency. 1977. xvii, 263 p. Based on files at the office of the Oregon State Registrar of Charitable Trusts and information supplied by the foundations. Main section arranged alphabetically by foundation within five subdivisions: General Purpose Foundations, Special Purpose Foundations, Student Aid Funds, Service Clubs, and National Foundations with an Active Interest in Oregon. Appendixes are as follows: A) Foundations Excluded from Guide, B) Oregon Foundations Having Assets of $500,000 or More in Most Recent Fiscal Year, C) Oregon Foundations Making Grants of $50,000 or More in Most Recent Fiscal Year, D) Regional Breakdown of Oregon Foundations, Other than Metropolitan Portland, E) Guide Personnel, F) Letter Introducing Foundation Questionnaire, G) Foundation Questionnaire, H) Foundation Research Form, I) Other Private Funding

Sources, J) Grants to Oregon Organizations from 1975 to August 1, 1977 by National Foundations Reporting on a Regular Basis to The Foundation Center, New York, K) Foundation Resource Centers and Bibliography, and L) Grant Retrieval Service. Index of foundation names. Available from Tri-County Community Council, 718 Burnside, Portland, Oregon 97209. $7.50 plus $.50 postage.

Pennsylvania (1078 foundations). *Directory of Pennsylvania Foundations.* 1st edition. Compiled by S. Damon Kletzien, editor, with assistance from Margaret H. Chalfant and Frances C. Ritchey. 1978. xvi, 304 p. Based on 1975 and 1976 990-PF and 990-AR returns filed with the IRS and information supplied by foundations. Main section arranged alphabetically within geographic regions. Appendixes on approaching foundations, program planning and proposal writing, and broadening the foundation search. Indexes of officers, directors and trustees; major interests; foundations arranged alphabetically. Available from Friends of the Free Library (Attn. Directory), The Free Library of Philadelphia, Logan Square at Nineteenth Street, Philadelphia, Pennsylvania 19103. $14.00 prepaid.

South Carolina (203 foundations). *South Carolina Foundation Directory.* 1st edition. Edited by Anne K. Middletown. 1978. 53 p. Based on 1975 990-PF and 990-AR returns filed with the IRS. Main section arranged alphabetically by foundation. Indexes by city and fields of interest. Available from Anne K. Middleton, Assistant Reference Librarian, South Carolina State Library, P.O. Box 11469, Columbia, South Carolina 29211. Send $.70 in postage stamps.

Texas (approximately 1370 foundations). *Directory of Texas Foundations.* 4th edition. Compiled and edited by William J. Hooper. 1980. vi, 184 p. Based on mostly 1978 and 1979 990-PF and 990-AR returns filed with the IRS. Main section arranged alphabetically by foundation. Also a section on dissolved foundations. Indexes of areas of interest and cities. Available from Texas Foundation Research Center, P.O. Box 5494, Austin, Texas 78763. Make check payable to: TFRC. $19.85 prepaid. Add $.90 for sales tax if applicable.

Texas (approximately 200 foundations). *The Guide to Texas Foundations.* 2nd edition. Edited by Jed Riffe. 1980. 103 p. Based on data from cooperating foundations and from 1977 and 1978 records in the Attorney-General's Office and the Dallas Public Library. Main section arranged alphabetically by city location of foundation. Covers foundations with grant totals over $30,000 per year. Index of foundations and areas of interest. Available from Marianne Cline, Dallas Public Library, 1954 Commerce Street, Dallas, Texas 75201. $10.00 prepaid.

Virginia (102 foundations). *Virginia Directory of Private Foundations*. By the Office of Human Resources, Department of Intergovernmental Affairs. 1977. 70 p. Based on 1974 and 1975 990-PF and 990-AR returns filed with the IRS. Main section arranged alphabetically by foundation. Indexes of foundations, geographical areas, and subjects. Available from Department of Intergovernmental Affairs, Fourth Street Office Building, 205 North Fourth Street, Richmond, Virginia 23219. $2.00 prepaid.

Washington (approximately 968 organizations). *Charitable Trust Directory*. (2nd edition). Compiled by the Office of the Attorney-General. 1980. 242 p. Based on 1979 records in the Washington Attorney-General's Office. Includes information on all charitable organizations and trusts reporting to the Attorney-General under the Washington Charitable Trust Act. Main section arranged alphabetically by organization. No indexes. Available from the Office of the Attorney-General, Temple of Justice, Olympia, Washington 98504. $4.00 prepaid.

West Virginia (approximately 99 foundations). *West Virginia Foundation Directory*. Compiled and edited by William Seeto. 1979. 49 p. Based on 1977 and 1978 990-PF and 990-AR returns filed with the IRS. Main section arranged alphabetically by foundation. Also a section on inactive or terminated foundations. Index by county and city. Available from West Virginia Foundation Directory, Box 96, Route 1, Terra Alta, West Virginia 26764. Make check payable to: West Virginia Foundation Directory. $7.95 prepaid.

Wisconsin (643 foundations). *Foundations in Wisconsin: A Directory 1980*. 4th edition. Compiled by Susan H. Hopwood. 1980. xiii, 271 p. Based on 1978 and 1979 990-PF and 990-AR returns filed with the IRS. Main section arranged alphabetically by foundation. Also sections listing inactive foundations, terminated foundations, and operating foundations. Indexes of areas of interest, counties, and foundation managers. Available from The Foundation Collection, Marquette University Memorial Library, 1415 West Wisconsin Avenue, Milwaukee, Wisconsin 53233. $12.50 prepaid plus $.48 sales tax or Wisconsin tax exempt number.

Glossary

applicant—individual, agency, or organization seeking funds

award—a grant

awarding agency—funding agency that makes a grant

award notice—formal written notification from a funding agency to a recipient, announcing that a grant has been awarded; also called "notice of grant award"

bidder's list—a list of qualified organizations maintained by government agencies for the purpose of sending organizations invitations to submit proposals and to bid on potential government contracts. Lists of bidders are used in determining to whom to send RFPs

block grant—a grant from a government funding source made as a total amount on the basis of some formula to a number of different recipients, often with relatively little control over its utilization. Revenue-sharing grants for certain general purposes are regarded as block grants

budget—itemized list of expenditures and income that accompanies a narrative proposal *budget period*—interval of time (usually twelve months) into which a grant-project period is divided for budgetary and reporting purposes

business proposal—used by some governmental grantors to refer to a separate proposal covering the budget and business aspects of the proposal, as distinguished from the technical or programmatic aspects of the proposal

capitation—payment per capita; used for a grant made to an organization on the basis of a given amount for each person enrolled or served, or potentially available to be served. The total amount of such a grant is the per capita amount granted multiplied by the number of persons served

Circular A-110—Office of Management and Budget (OMB) circular that sets forth the federal standards for financial-management systems to be maintained by organizations receiving federal funds

Commerce Business Daily—publication of Department of Commerce that announces availability of contracts (RFPs) and recipients of contract awards from the federal government

construction grant—grant made for and limited to construction, modernizing, or expanding a physical facility

contract—legal agreement between the grantee and grantor establishing the work to be performed, products to be delivered, time schedules, financial arrangements, and other provisions or conditions governing the arrangement

contractor—organization under a contract to the funder to perform specific work

cost overrun—difference between original estimated cost and the cumulative total of a cost-reimbursable contract

cost-plus contract—contract that provides for reimbursing the contractor for allowable costs that were incurred, plus a fixed fee or amount. Normally used with profit-making organizations; also known as cost-plus fixed-fee contract

cost proposal—separate proposal covering the budget, financial, and business aspects of the proposal; also called business proposal

cost-reimbursement contract—contract that provides for payment to the contractor on the basis of actual allowable costs or expenditures incurred in performing the scheduled work

cost sharing—arrangement whereby the grantee shares in the total cost of a project; required for many federal research programs

demonstration grant—grant made to support the demonstration and testing of the feasibility or piloting of a particular approach to service delivery, research, training, or technical assistance

direct assistance—grant under which goods and services are furnished in lieu of cash; it can be in the form of personnel, supplies, or equipment

direct costs—budget item that represents the direct expenditure of funds for salaries, fringe benefits, travel, equipment, supplies, communication, publications, and similar items

discretionary fund—government fund to be allocated by a federal agency, usually on the basis of competitive selection among a number of programs and purposes rather than according to any formula; the allocation results in contracts or grants

FAPRS—Federal Assistance Program Retrieval System, developed to provide local communities with information on federal programs

Federal Register—daily publication of the U.S. government that reports the rules and regulations governing various programs

fellowship—grant to support individual training to enhance the individual's level of competence in a particular field

FFP—federal financial participation

fixed-price contract—contract in which a fixed total amount is paid on the basis of delivery of a satisfactory product, regardless of the costs actually incurred by the contractor

formula grant—grant in which the funds are made available on the basis of a specific formula used by the granting agency and prescribed in legislation, regulations, or policies of that agency. Formula grants may make funds available on the basis of population characteristics (for example, two dollars for each person in a county age sixty-five and over), or on the basis of the proportion of the population in a certain area to that of the total population to be served (for example, ABC State represents 20 percent of the U.S. total population), or on the basis of numbers of people served (for example, twenty dollars for each person enrolled in a program)

fringe benefits—amount paid by the employer for various employee benefits such as social security, health insurance, retirement, and other insurances. Usually included in a budget as a percentage of total salaries

GANTT chart—timetable in chart form, showing the various activities included in a proposal, with indication of the length of time elapsing from the start to the end of each activity

grant—sum of money comprising an award of financial assistance to recipient individuals and organizations

grantee—individual, organization, or entity receiving a grant and responsible or accountable for that grant *grantor*—agency (government, foundation, corporation, nonprofit organization, individual) awarding a grant to a recipient

grant-supported activities/project—activities specified in a grant application, contract, letter of approval, or other document that are approved by a funding agency as the basis for awarding a grant

grants-management officer—official of a government funding agency or foundation who is designated as the responsible person for the business and financial aspects of a particular grant. This person is usually expected to work in collaboration with the grantor's program/project officer. The grants-management officer is the grantor's counterpart of the grantee's business and financial manager

guidelines—set of general principles specified as the basis for judging a proposal. Funder's guidelines specify which requirements the proposal must meet with respect to both its content and its form

indirect cost—budget item that represents costs incurred by the grantee in carrying out a program that are not readily identified as the direct expenditure of funds for goods and services, but which are necessary to facilitate and maintain the operations of the larger organizations sponsoring or carrying out the supported program. Examples are maintaining facilities, providing administration, and depreciation

in-kind contribution—dollar value of noncash contribution to a program by the grantee or a party other than the grantee or grantor. Such a contribution usually consists of contributed time of personnel, equipment, supplies, and rent that directly benefit the grant-supported activity

level of effort—estimated amount of time of personnel required to carry out a program, project, or activity usually expressed in man-years, -months, -weeks, -days, or -hours

local government—units of government below the state level such as counties, cities, towns, townships, school districts, and federally reorganized Indian tribal governments

local planning agencies—known as LPAs, these are agencies designated as the official responsible recipients for certain types of grants

maintenance of effort—requirement of some grantor programs that a grantee must maintain a specified level of activity and financial expenditures in a specified geographic or programmatic area in order to receive a grant. This is intended to assure that grant funds will not be used to replace or supplant funds already being expended by the grantee

man-years—indicates the level of effort to be expended. A sexist term, being replaced by "person-years" *matching*—participation by the grantee in the cost of a program on a dollar-for-dollar basis or other predetermined ratio or basis, such as 10 percent or 25 percent of the cost

milestones—timetable indicating the completion of the activities or events included in a proposal

notice of grant award—formal written notice from the grantor that specifies the amount of the grant, time period, and special requirements

990-AR—form of the annual reports that foundations submit to the Internal Revenue Service and to state attorneys general

offeror—organization that is submitting a proposal on and bidding on an RFP

person-years—used to indicate the level of effort of a given person or in the aggregate for an entire project in terms of years of work to be expended. For example, "The project will require a total of six person-years over a twelve-month period"

PERT—stands for Program Evaluation Review Technique, which is a schedule of events and activities included in a project indicating the period of time elapsing between events and the relationship of events to each other

planning grant—grant intended to support activities necessary to design and plan a particular program or project, to design and plan programs in a particular geographic area and/or a particular field of service, or to engage in interagency planning and coordination. Planning grants often include research, study, coordination, community participation, community organization, and education activities as components of the planning activities

principal investigator—see program director

prior approval—written permission from a granting agency (usually a governmental funder) for a grantee to expend funds or perform or modify certain activities when this is a requirement of the grantor. An approved budget is, in effect, prior approval; approval of a revised budget or written request to make program modifications is also a form of prior approval

program director—individual designated by the grantee to direct the program or project being supported by the grant. Also known as "project director" or "principal investigator." This person is responsible to the grantee organization for proper management and conduct of the project or program. The grantee organization is responsible to the grantor. In some unusual cases, however, project directors and principal investigators may be made directly accountable to grantors

program/project costs—direct and indirect cost incurred in carrying out a grant-supported program or project. In the case of some grantors, only the cost estimated in the approved budget may be incurred by the grantee as allowable expense related to the grant

program or project officers—usually refers to the official in a governmental funding agency or in a foundation who is responsible within that agency for a grant project or program. In some cases this person may, in addition to supervision of technical and program aspects of the grants, be responsible for administrative and financial aspects of the grant. This latter function is more frequently the responsibility, at least in federal agencies, of a second person (called the grants-management officer)

program/project period—total time over which the grant is to be expended

proposal—formal written document that provides detailed information to a funder on the proposed conduct and cost of a specific program or project

reimbursement formula—basis for a grantor providing funds to a grantee in cases where funds are to be granted according to some formula related to population, services rendered, or proportion of the budget to be shared by the grantee

research grant—grant to support research in the form of studies, surveys, evaluations, investigations, and experimentation

revenue sharing—federal program providing more or less automatic federal assistance to states and localities for broad general purposes and with limited federal control

RFP—stands for "Request for Proposal," which is a formal announcement from a funding agency inviting the submission of a proposal and specifying the requirements that the proposal must meet with respect to the objectives, scope of work, work plan, administration, timing, and reporting. An RFP usually results in a contract as the mechanism for conveying the funds and sets forth the specific products that are to result from the program or project

site visit—visit by one or more persons responsible to the funding agency to the site of the submitter of a proposal in order to obtain additional evaluative information on the basis of firsthand observation and discussion

solicited proposal—proposal that responds to an RFP or a formal invitation of a funder

sole source—agency or organization considered by the funder to be the only available resource to fulfill the requirements of a proposed contract *stipend*—payment to an individual, usually as part of a training or fellowship program

technical proposal—used by some governmental grantors to refer to the narrative proposal that covers all aspects of the proposal except the budget and financial and business information (which is to be included in a separate business proposal)

third party—organization or individual other than the grantee or grantor who is involved in a supported program

training grant—grant to support training of staff, students, prospective employees, program participants, or designated populations

unobligated balance—amount remaining of a grant at the end of the grant period against which there will be no expenses. Such balances, at the discretion of the grantor, may have to be returned, or they may be used as a deduction from the next grant (a continuation) if there is one, or carried over to the next continuation period as an addition to the next grant

unsolicited proposal—proposal sent to a government foundation or other funding source that is initiated by the applicant

wired—term indicating that the selection of an organization to receive a grant has been decided prior to the submission of competitive proposals

Index